Following Christ

Following Christ

MODELS *of* DISCIPLESHIP
in the NEW TESTAMENT

ANDREW RYDER, S.C.J.

SHEED & WARD

Franklin, Wisconsin

As an apostolate of the Priests of the Sacred Heart, a Catholic religious order, the mission of Sheed & Ward is to publish books of contemporary impact and enduring merit in Catholic Christian thought and action. The books published, however, reflect the opinions of their authors and are not meant to represent the official position of the Priests of the Sacred Heart.

1999

Sheed & Ward
7373 South Lovers Lane Road
Franklin, Wisconsin 53132
1-800-266-5564

Printed in the United States of America

Cover design: Madonna Gaulding

Interior design: GrafixStudio, Inc.

Scripture quotations are from the New Revised Standard Version of the Bible, copyright 1989 by the Division of Christian Education of the National Council of the Churches of Christ in the USA. Used by permission. All rights reserved.

Library of Congress Cataloging-in-Publication Data

Ryder, Andrew.
    Following Christ : models of discipleship in the New Testament / by Andrew Ryder.
        p. cm.
    ISBN 1-58051-068-X (alk. paper)
    1. Bible. N.T.—Criticism, interpretation, etc. 2. Christian life—Biblical teaching. I. Title.
    BS2545. C48 R93 1999
    248' .09' 015—dc21   99-36301
                                            CIP

1 2 3 4 5 / 02 01 00 99

To the memory of
Bill and Sarah Ryder,
my parents

*"Christ is like a rich mine with many recesses containing
treasures, and no matter how we try to fathom them the end is
never reached. Rather, in each recess, we keep on finding here
and there new veins of new riches."*

St. John of the Cross

The Grace to Walk Beside You

The grace to walk beside you on the Way
is what I ask of you, my Lord, today:
to be with you no matter what the Hour;
to face each task enlightened by your Power.   [Luke 24:49]

I chase and think the things which are absurd   [Mark 8: 33]
and fail to hear your liberating Word.
Thus human glory forms a heart unfree   [John 12:42–43]
by forcing me from where I first would be.

"Oh Son of David stop! Please pass not by.   [Mark 10:46–52]
In your sweet mercy stay, and heed my cry."
The world may mock and sneer. Let it be so.
With blinded grip I shall not let you go

but sink before your presence to my knees,
refusing a denial of my pleas.
My heart's desire now clamors for its say:
the grace to walk beside you on the Way.

Because the Holy Mother takes my part
—she is the final blessing of your Heart—   [John 19:26–27]
the answer to this prayer will not be Nay:
the grace to walk beside you on the Way.

I sit expectant in the Banquet Hall.
You speak of single grains; of seeds that fall;   [John 12:24–25]
of those who die to self; who others serve.
These seek but you, so life, through death, preserve.

You gently lay your hand upon my head.
I remember what you said about the Bread:
"through This you will be given, come what may,   [John 6:56–57]
the grace to walk beside me on the Way."

—Andrew Ryder, S.C.J.

Table of Contents

Preface

The turning point of George Eliot's masterpiece, *Middle-march*, takes place when Dorothea Casaubon discovers that her husband is unwilling to use the new methods of historical research. In a spirit of self-sacrifice she had married him so that together they could dedicate their future to the study of classical literature. When she hears that Casaubon is unwilling to follow the leads of contemporary scholars she becomes "startled and anxious." She has received an inkling that her husband's survey of the ancient world is going nowhere. He is wandering around, lost in the woods, ignoring the roads opened up by "competent scholars."

I mention this episode in *Middlemarch* for two reasons. First, by the time George Eliot was writing in the nineteenth century, great strides had been made in the study of ancient texts. These gains were closely linked to the vast amount of research into the background of the Old and New Testaments. By 1870 the major problems of New Testament study that we are grappling with today had been identified.

Second, as Dorothea was advised, we too have to avoid "groping around in the woods," neglecting to follow the good roads already marked out if we want to benefit fully from the message of the Scriptures. Even though such study will not, of itself, make us more docile to the Word of God, a better understanding of the text can at least help us to identify more clearly what the Word of God is saying.

We are fortunate in our time to be able to call upon a host of "competent scholars" when we seek to interpret the message of the New Testament. The twentieth century has been a golden age of Scripture studies. Not only have we had an abundance of translations of the original texts, we have also been blessed with commentators of outstanding caliber giving us the fruits of their labors.

One of the valuable gains of recent study has been a clearer awareness that the New Testament is not a single book, but a collection, a veritable library of books. Each one has its own special history, with a particular character, style, and purpose. Although all the books derive from the life and teaching of Jesus Christ, they look at his message from different angles and situations. Sometimes the differences between even the four Gospels are quite extensive, as a comparison between John and Mark will instantly make clear.

An approach to the New Testament writings based on their differing historical backgrounds is the basis of what has come to be known as *redaction criticism:* The study of the various stages (redactions) of New Testament composition. Unlike the earlier forms of research that concentrated on individual units of the scriptural text, redaction criticism tries to identify the purpose and vision of each book taken as a whole. By examining the historical setting of a particular writer, the redaction critic tries to identify his particular concerns. This helps us to see how the original message has been adapted to the needs of a particular time and circumstance. This varying background leads to the different points of view and styles in the New Testament. The message is presented by each author within a specific historical milieu.

Redaction criticism is particularly helpful in the study of the Gospels. The Gospel writers were not merely collectors of traditions but individual composers. "Each has his own special message and that message can be gauged from the way he selects, structures, and collects his material into the total framework of the Gospel."[1]

Like most other Christian institutions, the Catholic Church was at first cautious in accepting the new methods of biblical interpretation. However, this attitude had changed by the time the Second Vatican Council began in 1962. The Council's *Constitution on Divine Revelation* proposed an approach to God's revelation based on the notion of a historical process. A subsequent Vatican instruction dealt specifically with redaction criticism. It reminded scholars of the different perspectives adopted by the evangelists:

> They selected certain things out of the many which had been handed on; some they synthesized, some they explained with an eye to the situation of the Churches, painstakingly using every means of bringing home to their readers the solid truth of the things in which they had been instructed. For, out of the material which they had received, the sacred authors selected especially those items which were adapted to the varied circumstances of the faithful as well as to the end which they themselves wished to attain; these they recounted in a manner consonant with those circumstances and with that end.[2]

The Letters of St. Paul are the first layer of the New Testament. Composed between A.D. 50 and 58, they are the oldest testimony we have to the faith of the early Christians. As we shall see, Paul was not primarily interested in the details of Jesus' earthly life. Apart from the death of Jesus on the cross, Paul says little and gives us no information about the historical Jesus of Nazareth. Paul was concerned about Jesus' teaching and the meaning of his death and resurrection for the Christian believer.

Although for a long time Christians saw the Gospels as a factual record of what happened, we now see them more as community documents based on the life and teaching of

Jesus. They adapt the form and even the wording of his message to the local situation and its individual needs. A clearer understanding of the origins of the Gospels, and an awareness of their purpose as documents of faith, have made us realize that they are not to be taken as day-by-day accounts of the life of Jesus.

Written in the last part of the first century, the Gospels are literary compositions. They are based on the oral traditions and (probably) written fragments that were in circulation from the beginning. Each Gospel, including that of Mark, was a theological composition. The prime concern of the evangelists was not precise historical accuracy in our sense of the term. The Gospels were compositions based on the life and teaching of Jesus, which applied his message to the needs of the early communities.

So the New Testament books are not precise historical records. Rather they are attestations of faith. At the same time, the faith of the community was not produced out of nothing. The early Christian communities were the result of actual events. They looked to Jesus Christ for the meaning of their existence. We can reach back, in some measure, to the Jesus of history as well as to the early Christian communities through the records of those who have given literary expression to their faith.

Though the Gospels and the other books of the New Testament are essentially faith documents, there is, of necessity, an essential historical core of fact underlying them. The theory of an unbridgeable gap between "the Jesus of history" and "the Christ of faith" fails to see that faith and history are intimately connected and, in the Christian view, cannot be radically opposed to each other.

The Jesus of history also called people to commit themselves in faith to follow him. He often admonished his disciples on account of the weakness of their faith. On the other hand, the Christ in whom we believe today is known to us only through the historical community that draws its inspiration from him. Without this necessary historical link, the Lord in whom we believe would be unknown to us.[3]

The theme of this book is the following of Christ. Discipleship is a subject of perennial interest for the committed Christian. One of the most popular creations in the history of spirituality was Thomas à Kempis's fifteenth-century *Imitation of Christ.* Even if the *Imitation* has long since disappeared from the best-selling list, the subject matter retains all its importance and attractiveness today.

As we celebrate the beginning of the third millennium the time seems ripe to look at this topic again. Now as much as ever we need to locate our faith in a commitment to Jesus Christ. Without denying the legitimacy of the developments that have taken place over the course of twenty centuries, we have to go back to the privileged sources of the New Testament.

My aim is to present the following of Christ according to the different traditions of the New Testament. The first writer of the New Testament is Paul, and so the first chapter looks at the meaning of Christian discipleship in Paul's Letters. Then, of course, there are the Gospels, and I begin with Mark, generally accepted today as the first of the evangelist writers, and proceed to Matthew, Luke, and John, whose writings followed Mark. After the Gospels, I have taken other representatives of the tradition, including Hebrews and the Book of Revelation.

The writings of the New Testament do not present a single concept of discipleship. They are compositions that contain a complex cluster of traditions and sayings. What I have attempted is to highlight the salient characteristics of each tradition and relate them to complementary approaches in the other writings. In this way I hope to illustrate discipleship from different angles and give a more complete presentation of the theme.

Conscious of the scope of the task that I have set for myself, and aware of the many difficulties that lie in the exposition of this theme, I make my own the prayer of St. Hilary as he began his treatise on the mystery of the Trinity. Addressing God he said:

In our need we shall pray for those things which we lack, and shall apply ourselves with determined zeal to the study of the words of your prophets and apostles, and we shall knock at every door where knowledge is locked in. But it is for you to bestow what is prayed for, and to be there when we seek; and to open when we knock.[4]

Finally, I would like to thank the staff of the Biblical Institute Library, Rome, for its courtesy and assistance during the academic year 1996–97, and Margaret Hammerot, for carefully editing the final text.

—Andrew Ryder
May 31, 1999
Feast of the Visitation

ONE

Conversion and Commitment

The Religious Experience of Paul

Abraham and Moses, the twin pillars of the Old Testament, experienced a personal call from God that resulted in a great change. Each of their conversion stories is linked to journeys. Abraham had to leave his native land; Moses was in flight from the Pharaoh when he encountered God in the burning bush.

The New Testament speaks about Paul's conversion in a similar way. He too was on a journey when he experienced the call to be an apostle of Jesus Christ. He was on his way to Damascus with the objective of destroying the Christian church there when suddenly his preconceptions were shattered in a moment of dazzling illumination. As he said later: *"God, who had set me apart before I was born and called me through his grace, was pleased to reveal his Son to me"* (Gal 1:15–16).

Paul's conversion marked a complete change of attitude. This event was the foundation on which his whole later career as an apostle was built. Nobody in the early church matched the breadth of Paul's vision or the depth of his theological penetration. Nobody traveled as much as he did. Nobody else was so effectively able to plant the message of Christ in the pagan cities of the day. As the greatest thinker of the first Christian generation, Paul saw more clearly and expressed more forcibly than the other apostles the implications of Christ's resurrection. As a result of Paul's efforts the Christian movement burst out of its narrow Jewish origins and became a world religion. All this flowed from his experience of conversion.

Although the Acts of the Apostles is the earliest history of the church and gives a great deal of space to Paul, it was written long after his death. Therefore, our best source for understanding Paul is his correspondence. In his Letters, Paul gives us a first-hand account of what the Lord Jesus Christ meant for him. They are the first body of Christian writing and some of them precede the composition of Mark's earliest Gospel by as many as twenty years. Thus they form the first layer of the New Testament and are the bedrock of its message.

Even though the conversion of Paul was the beginning of his career as an apostle, it was not the start of his life of commitment to God. Paul brought to this encounter other experiences. The gifts and talents he had already formed were put to good use in his new task.

Paul came to Damascus as a child of two worlds: Jewish and Roman. The most important formative elements he brought to bear on his encounter with the risen Christ are summed up in the two names he bore: Saul and Paul—like many Jews of the period Paul had both a Semitic and a Roman name. His two names are indicative of his experience in the world and his relationship with God.[1]

"I myself am an Israelite, a descendant of Abraham, a member of the tribe of Benjamin" (Rom 11:1)

Paul's Jewish birthright remained precious to him. Although his conversion made him see the institutions of his old faith in a new light, he never renounced the basic elements of his heritage. He was always aware of his background and happily professed his membership in the race chosen by God.

As an Israelite, Paul was part of the people to whom belonged the glory, the covenant, the law, the cult, and the promises (Rom 9:4). He was from the tribe of Benjamin, the clan of the youngest son of Jacob and the one beloved by him. From this tribe came Saul, the first king of Israel, after whom the (later) Apostle Paul was most likely named.

In addition, Paul was a Pharisee and proud of it. Being a member of that sect marked him as a person of deep commitment to the Jewish law with zeal for the traditions of the fathers. He excelled his peers "in Judaism" (Gal 1:14). Through his strict observance of the Mosaic law, Paul lived as a young man in the spiritual world of the Old Testament and venerated the God who had spoken through the prophets. This did not change after his conversion: The God of the fathers continued to be his God and he often expressed himself in Old Testament terms. For example, his way of quoting Scripture stayed similar to that of the Jewish rabbis; he used their techniques in Romans chapters 9 to 11, where he discusses the role of the Jewish nation in God's plan of salvation.

In many ways Paul remained a first-century Jew even after becoming a Christian. His journey of faith was deeply rooted in the religion of his youth and he was always to stress the unity of God's plan. What happened in the first covenant with Abraham was God's way of preparing for the coming of his Son. If Paul contrasted the letter of the law to the spirit, he still believed that what was written for Abraham continued to be relevant for the disciples of Jesus.

"I am a Jew, from Tarsus in Cilicia, a citizen of an important city" (Acts 21:39)

Paul was not a Jew from Palestine. He belonged to what was known as the *Diaspora*, the community of Jews spread throughout the world. His cultural background is revealed by his Roman name, his quotations from the Greek version of the Old Testament, and the fact that he wrote his Letters in Greek. In other words, Paul was very much a child of the

Greco-Roman world. Specifically, according to Acts 21:39, he was a Jew from Tarsus (modern southern Turkey).

Tarsus was a city famous in the ancient world for its intellectual tradition and this education shines out in Paul. His literary style and way of composing letters follow the models of Greek rhetoric, which is especially evident in his Letters to the Galatians and the Romans. Moreover, he wrote in the classical mode—an indication of the care he took in presenting the Christian message.

Whereas Jesus used images from the country life of Galilee to illustrate his teaching, and spoke in parables that often took their inspiration from a rural setting, Paul was more at home in the city. He used Greek political terms, alluded to Greek games, and employed Greek commercial terminology. His understanding of the community as "the body of Christ" (1 Cor 12:27–28) almost certainly reflects the political language of the day.

Paul's contacts with contemporary culture were decisive influences on his presentation of the good news. He could not have written about the problems of faith as he did if he had not first had to cope with the needs of converts from pagan society. Astride the two worlds of Judea and Rome, he was in a unique position to make the vital connections between one culture and the other. But it was not all one-way traffic across that bridge. Paul learned from his converts as well and could admit at the end that he was also *"a debtor both to Greeks and to barbarians"* (Rom 1:14).

To fully appreciate Paul, we must first address a vital question:

What Happened on the Road to Damascus?

There are three accounts of Paul's conversion in the Acts of the Apostles, which shows how central a position the event occupied in the mind of Luke, the author of Acts and the first "church historian." Indeed, after the life, death, and resurrection of Jesus, the most important fact in the New Testament is the conversion of Paul. He played the key role in transforming Christianity from a sect within Judaism into a world religion. Consequently Luke's Acts of the Apostles, with its concern for the growth of the Christian movement, puts Paul center stage.

While in his Letters Paul described his experience on the road to Damascus as a "seeing" without any words being spoken, Luke composed a dialogue between Jesus and Paul that is consistent in all three accounts: *"Saul, Saul, why do you persecute me?" "Who are you, Lord?" "I am Jesus, whom you are persecuting."* In this way Luke underlined a central theme of his history of the early Christian community: The identification between the risen Lord Jesus Christ and the church.

Many scholars dispute the exact historical value of these accounts in Acts. What does seem certain is that at the time of Paul's conversion, Christians still considered themselves to be Jews. The first Christians did not see their faith in Jesus as a different religion; they were Jews with a new vision of what it meant to be part of God's people.

But to the rest of the Jewish world, the followers of Christ were an aberration, a deviation from the purity of the faith. So the measures taken against them were considered a necessary defense of traditional Jewish belief. In the stern and rigorous view of the unconverted Paul, any deviation from the Law was totally unacceptable. Such activity endangered the traditions of his people and had to be rooted out with all the force available.

On the basis of their faith in Christ, the Christian Jews at Damascus were probably admitting Gentiles into their community without demanding that they undergo the rite of circumcision. But for people like Paul, maintaining this practice was essential. There was no way baptism could ever be accepted as a substitute for such an ancient and hallowed institution. Paul considered it imperative to bring these Christian Jews into line.

None of the available evidence suggests that Paul was starting to doubt the validity of his Jewish beliefs or was beginning to waver in his allegiance to his faith. There is nothing in his Letters to suggest that he had a lengthy struggle with conversion or that the episode at Damascus was merely the final step of a process already long at work.

In other words, we find no gradual weakening of Paul's opposition to Christianity. Quite the contrary, his journey to Damascus was inspired by vehement anti-Christian sentiments—he was intent on destroying what he saw as a dangerous heretical movement. In fact, it was the sudden contrast, the complete transformation, that became for the later Paul the clearest sign that God had truly met him on the Damascus road. He had received such overwhelming evidence of the lordship of Jesus Christ that he had to let go of his hostility to Jesus' followers.

In his Letters Paul shows no interest in any psychological probing of his conversion experience. He judges his meeting with Christ by the actions it inspired and by the impetus his life received. He does not give a detailed description of what actually happened. Using the terminology of the Old Testament prophets, he says that he was called to be the Apostle to the Gentiles. That God had called him was beyond any doubt.

"Last of all, as to one untimely born, he appeared also to me" (1 Cor 15:8)

Paul's powerful sense of vocation is expressed in those parts of his Letters where he exerts his authority. Above all, he strongly defends himself when he feels his right to be considered an apostle is disputed. Like the Twelve, Paul claims to be a witness of the risen Lord, though he is ready to admit that he is *"one untimely born"* (1 Cor 15:8). He describes his conversion experience in different ways: He has *seen* the Lord (1 Cor 9:1); Christ *appeared* to him (1 Cor 15:8); and God *revealed* his Son to him (Gal 1:16).

In the accounts of the Damascus event given by Paul himself there is no reference to any voice or words being spoken. Even when he mentions some kind of vision, what is of ultimate significance is not the mode of perception, but rather the fruits of his experience. The vision is the manner of commissioning. The call to be an apostle is of most significance.

Paul was primarily concerned with the task that was given to him, not the historical details of his encounter with the Lord. Consequently it is very difficult to know what precisely happened on the road to Damascus. What is indisputable, however, is that from then on everything changed in Paul's life. So complete was the reversal in his view of the world and in his traditional spiritual practices that he could say that he no longer lived himself, but that Christ lived in him (Gal 2:19).

Paul nowhere mentions hearing any words spoken. He only describes a visionary happening. But if Christ did not speak to him, certain questions arise: How could he have grasped so much and experienced a drastic change of perception in such a short space of time? How could all that have been the result merely of a vision, without any words of explanation being given to him?

Answers to these questions can only be discovered by looking at the situation in which Paul found himself at the time of his conversion. Paul does this himself when he speaks of his former zeal for the law and his persecution of Christian believers.

The people who were the objects of Paul's vengeance were breaking away from the Jewish law. They based their new liberty on a belief in the resurrection of Jesus. Despite his hostility, indeed as the very precondition of his persecution, Paul was aware of the Christian viewpoint. Now, in the act of trying to root out belief in the one he considered a traitor to the faith, Paul himself had a vision of the resurrected Christ.

The one on whom Christians based their illegalities was alive. God had truly raised the crucified Jesus, whom his followers regarded as risen. This fact was impressed upon Paul in an unmistakable fashion. In one flash of insight everything else fell into place: The claims of the disciples of Jesus were based on truth.

This sudden revelation had enormous implications for Paul. If God had raised and exalted Jesus in such a manner and proclaimed him to be his Son, then Paul's stance was wrong. It would have to be completely reviewed. Paul's vision of Christ in glory resulted therefore in a fundamental change of perspective. In one instant he realized that far from being an outcast and a deceiver, Jesus was the channel of God's salvation for the world.

The conversion, which brought about Paul's new frame of mind, also made a difference to his lifestyle. As we find in the case of many Old Testament prophets, Isaiah for example, the experience of the divine presence was not only a revelation but also a commissioning. The vision of the Risen One changed Paul's understanding of Christ and his own manner of living. Henceforth he was called to proclaim to others the meaning of the revelation. He too would be an apostle of the Easter Jesus.

The church Paul had started out to destroy now became the recipient of his energy, intellectual gifts, and organizational ability. Given the type of person Paul was, he could not just go home from Damascus to continue his trade as a tentmaker and lead a comfortable life. He could not leave to others the task of proclaiming the gospel of Jesus Christ. He too would have to build up the Christian community as an apostle. His endeavors would make him the Apostle to the Gentiles.

Defending his right to be an apostle, Paul cries out: *"Am I not an apostle? Have I not seen Jesus our Lord?"* (1 Cor 9:1). Others challenged Paul's claim. There were those who reserved the prestigious title "apostle" strictly to the ones who had walked with the earthly Jesus. In their view Paul did not meet the criteria that had been laid down in the selection of a replacement for Judas (Acts 1:17).

But for Paul the only difference between himself and the Twelve was a temporal one: His vision of the risen Jesus took place later than those of the "official" witnesses. Paul was convinced that his experience put him on the same footing as the others: *". . . God, who had set me apart before I was born and called me through his grace, was pleased to reveal his Son to me, so that I might proclaim him among the Gentiles"* (Gal 1:15–16). We cannot say of Paul that he had the experience but missed the meaning. His whole life was spent reflecting on it. Yet what happened to Paul did not change his basic perception of God. The God who was worshiped by the fathers now showed himself to be the Father of Jesus Christ. The divine Creator of the world who promised to save his people, despite their infidelities, had now intervened decisively in the person of his Son.

What changed for Paul was his understanding of Jesus Christ. This is what gave the vision on the road to Damascus such importance. The passion and death of Jesus were now seen in an entirely different light: *"But we proclaim Christ crucified, a stumbling block to Jews and foolishness to Gentiles, but to those who are the called, both Jews and Greeks, Christ the power of God and the wisdom of God"* (1 Cor 1:23–24).

The full extent of Paul's experience was not totally clear to him at the moment of conversion. Time, reflection, and controversy would be needed to deepen his insight into the mystery of Christ. Paul's on-going mission, together with learning the church tradition that preceded him, were factors that enabled him to fashion an interpretation of Christianity that was to be distinctively his own. Further reflection was also imposed upon him through the need to explain the message of Jesus to his converts.

Yet, in all essentials, the change took place at the moment of his conversion. Everything that happened afterwards and all that was written by Paul to the various communities stem from that one moment of illumination. His experience near Damascus was not just the turning point in his own personal life: It was also to have a decisive effect on the community to which he committed himself. Through his preaching and his writing he became the chief interpreter of the gospel, the founder of churches, and the first Christian theologian.

Paul referred to his own journey of faith as an example for others. His devotion to Christ and his wholehearted commitment to his God-given task were reference points for other disciples. If not precisely in the manner, Paul's calling could be taken as a model for all the followers of Jesus. Every man and woman could be transformed through an encounter with the risen Lord.

"And you became imitators of us and of the Lord" (1 Thess 1:6).

Paul made clear to the readers of the First Letter to the Thessalonians (1:6) that he offered a pattern for his converts to follow. The life of grace, which had come to him through his meeting with Christ, had also been bestowed upon them in baptism. They too were called to reflect on the nature of their experience and to work out its implications for their daily Christian existence.

"I know a person in Christ who fourteen years ago was caught up to the third heaven—whether in the body or out of the body I do not know; God knows" (2 Cor 12:2). The ecstasy Paul speaks about in 2 Corinthians is not related to what happened on the road to Damascus. Paul did not consider this later event, unlike the vision that brought about his conversion, of any great significance. He did not seem to believe it had much value for his apostolic career or his Christian life. The rapture is not referred to in other parts of his Letters. This has led some scholars to conclude that it was a single phenomenon, never to be repeated.

Paul spoke of the ecstasy unwillingly and only because the charismatic disciples in Corinth held such mystical favors in high esteem. Paul, in fact, minimized the importance of his rapture by putting it in a cloud of incomprehension. Much more significant for Paul were the sufferings and labors he endured for the sake of Christ crucified: *"So, I will boast all the more gladly of my weaknesses, so that the power of Christ may dwell in me"* (2 Cor 12:9).

Against the tendency of the church at Corinth to emphasize the significance of mystical knowledge and undervalue the witness of the cross, Paul had already in his

First Letter to the Corinthians recalled them to the concrete obligations of the Christian life. He had urged his converts not to consider themselves an elitist group. Rather they were to assume a role of humble service within the church (chapters 11–14).

Paul therefore referred to his ecstasy in a very guarded way. He realized that too much concern for unusual spiritual experiences could give rise to overconfidence and, even worse, divisions within the Christian community.

Paul's Appeal to Experience

Through the startling nature of his conversion, Paul realized that the resurrection of Christ had had a profound impact on the traditional practices of his faith. Henceforth allegiance to Christ, not the observance of external norms and customs, would be the decisive factor in the eyes of God. Paul appealed to his vision of the risen Christ to prove that converts from paganism were not bound by all the rules of the Jewish religion. Even though Christian Jews might continue to observe the rite of circumcision and laws about food, such practices were no longer obligatory.

Not all agreed with him. Many still considered themselves bound to follow the old laws concerning food and circumcision. These conflicting views threatened to separate Paul from the more traditional members of the church. In his Letter to the Galatians (his second Epistle probably written between A.D. 52 and 54) Paul expressed for the first time what would be a central theme of his preaching and writing: The freedom of the Christian from the burden of the law.

Paul had spent some time evangelizing the people of Galatia (in modern Turkey) and had passed on to them his views on the matter of Jewish legal observance. After Paul's departure the Christian community in Galatia was visited by a group of missionaries who insisted on circumcision and observance of other time-honored customs.

The newly formed Christian community in Galatia was thrown into confusion by these conflicting instructions.

Someone most likely sent word to Paul for clarification; hence the sharp tone of Paul's Letter to the Galatians. Concern that his converts were being deflected from their first instruction added to his sense of grievance that his integrity as an apostle was being questioned. Galatians is the most personally revealing of Paul's writings.

The first two chapters are autobiographical. Paul speaks of his conversion as a moment of revelation in which he was commissioned to be the Apostle to the Gentiles. The direct and personal nature of the revelation he received, as well as the fact that he was totally unprepared for the message, are given as proofs of its divine origin.

Paul goes on to relate the story of his meeting with the other apostles in Jerusalem (2:1–10). He found to his satisfaction that the "pillar apostles" accepted the divine origin of his preaching: *"They saw that I had been entrusted with the gospel for the uncircumcised, just as Peter had been entrusted with the gospel for the circumcised"* (2:7).

Paul's meeting with the apostles and their positive response to his preaching were important moments in his missionary career. He was judged by them to be a faithful exponent of the gospel. As a result, his encounter with the Lord on the way to Damascus was given official approval. We see in this episode that Paul was not a free agent in his interpretation of the gospel. He too had to conform to the rule of faith that was already in force before his conversion.

The divine origin of Paul's gospel had already, in one important sense, been validated by the fruitfulness of his apostolic labors. But there was still need for the confirmation of the Twelve. Paul informs his readers that the "so-called pillars" gave him the right hand of fellowship and recognized the grace that had been given to him (2:9). However wryly described, this approval of the apostles was crucial for his mission. Without it he would have been a lone voice, operating without any authentic mandate.

Paul's need for confirmation (*"to make sure that I was not running, or had not run, in vain,"* see Phil 2:16) indicates how important the validation of the church was for him. He considered the attitude of the community to be a decisive factor in assessing the truth of an individual's position. He took the same approach when dealing with a dissident group of charismatics in his Letters to the Corinthians.

Paul goes on to relate the painful and humiliating incident of his confrontation with Peter at Antioch.[2] He wanted the Galatians, now in danger of abandoning the message he had preached, to realize how strongly he supported their freedom from the obligations of the Jewish observance. He was asking them to discern for themselves the strength of his conviction and how determined he was to defend what he believed to be the truth.

Paul pursues his argument by a further call to the experience of his readers: *"Well then, does God supply you with the Spirit and work miracles among you by your doing the works of the law, or by your believing what you heard?"* (3:5). Paul was asking the Galatians to reflect on what had happened when, as a result of his preaching, they accepted the message of faith.[3] The active presence of the Spirit was a clear indication that they had made the right move. A return to the old ways would mean that the Spirit had been received to no purpose.

Every expression of the Spirit's gifts is not under scrutiny here. The area of experience Paul appeals to is the prayer life of his Galatian converts. The sense of being a child of God is the crucial test: *"God has sent the Spirit of his Son into our hearts, crying, 'Abba! Father!'"* (4:6). The Spirit's cry is of an intensity that comes right from the heart of the disciple. The spontaneity and emotional depth of the prayer are indications of its genuine nature. Paul regarded the prayer of the Christian as an echo of Jesus' own prayer. Those who pleaded with God in such a manner were giving a proof of their participation in the divine life of Jesus.

The retention of the Aramaic term *Abba* in the prayer is significant. There was a perfectly acceptable Greek form for the word *Father.* But the retention of the original Aramaic here, as in the Gospel accounts of Jesus' prayer, indicates that *Abba* was the characteristic way Jesus addressed God.

Consequently Paul was saying to the Galatians that the Spirit of the Son prolongs the prayer of the Son and so ratifies the faith of those who are praying.

"So you are no longer a slave but a child, and if a child then also an heir" (2 Cor 4:7)

Paul compares the Christian disciple to an adopted son in Roman law. Even though there was little external difference between the situation of a young son and a slave (because both were under the jurisdiction of the head of the household), the status of a slave could not be compared to that of the son. The great difference was the inheritance the son would receive. The same is true of Christian disciples. Through receiving the Spirit of the first-born Son, their status has been transformed from one of slavery to that of God's children. They have now come into their inheritance.

Paul's appeal to experience is not limited to the Galatians. All the followers of Jesus, through their membership in the Christian community, have received the Spirit. Paul moves from a discussion of the particular issue at stake to give an all-embracing vision of the church : *"There is no longer slave or free, there is no longer male and female; for all of you are one in Christ Jesus"* (3:28).

The last two chapters of Galatians balance out what has gone before by referring to the moral demands made on the disciples of Christ. Their deliverance from the bondage of the old ceremonial prescriptions does not mean that they are exempt from God's commandments. They have not been given the option to live in any way they please. Paul does not dispute the Ten Commandments and their demands on Christian living. His position is that without the grace of Christ, no human effort can make a person acceptable to God.

There may appear to be a certain retracing of steps by Paul in his concluding stress on the moral obligations of the Christian life. But if there is some inconsistency, Paul does not seem aware of any backtracking on the defense of

Christian freedom he had so strenuously mounted in the body of the Epistle.

This ambiguity touches on the nature of Paul's correspondence. His Letters do not set out to give a comprehensive treatment of doctrine. They deal with specific issues that have arisen in the community. Like any good teacher, Paul stresses that aspect of the problem being neglected by his readers.

Furthermore we have to remember that Paul himself was often working out his ideas as questions arose. Galatians is the first time he deals with what became a central issue of his theology: The relationship of the Christian disciple to the Old Testament. When compared to the later and much more elaborate Letter to the Romans, Galatians shows that additional reflection on the matter was still needed.

"Bear one another's burdens, and in this way you will fulfill the law of Christ" (Gal 6:2)

To uphold the basic requirements of morality and at the same time preserve what he has written about deliverance from the law, Paul appeals to the example of Jesus. Paul had already said that God's Son put himself under the law in order to redeem those under the law. In the life of Jesus Christ, we see freedom from what is merely human in religion together with a total commitment to God's will.

Paul's exhortation is grounded in his understanding of Jesus as the one who leads, who saves and who, by his fidelity to the point of death, gives us the possibility to live as true children of God. The law of Christ is therefore that manner of living that should flow spontaneously from the disciple's union with Christ.

We are delivered from sin through the faithfulness of Jesus. His fidelity is the example that the followers of Christ have to imitate. The same argument is used when Paul calls upon the Philippians to practice humility. He puts before them the self-emptying of the Son of God as the model of behavior. Christian morality is, above all, the imitation of Jesus.

The ideal of the imitation of Christ, developed later in the Christian tradition, finds an early expression in the Pauline Letters. In his First Letter to the Thessalonians, Paul commended his converts because they had become imitators of him and of the Lord (1:6). In his Letter to the Galatians this theme comes to the fore again. Paul sees Christian morality as first and foremost an imitation of Jesus. Such a pattern of life reveals the union of the disciple with Christ and the power of the Holy Spirit.

Several passages in Galatians give us a clear indication that Paul saw his own way of life as an imitation of Jesus. The best known is his identification with the sufferings of his crucified Lord: *"I have been crucified with Christ; and it is no longer I who live, but it is Christ who lives in me. And the life I now live in the flesh I live by faith"* (2:19–20).

In this passage Paul underscores the faith of the Son of God. Past commentators took it for granted that Paul intended "faith" to mean the belief of the disciple in Christ; that is, we are saved by *our* faith in Christ. More recently many scholars have become convinced that what is meant by the original Greek phrase is the faith *of the Son of God.* This is a more literal rendering of the original text. In this interpretation we are saying that by his faithfulness, by his fidelity even to death, Jesus has saved us. This is most likely what Paul means when he says we are saved by the faith of Jesus Christ.

Paul saw the hopes of the world realized in Christ. The perfection of Christ's love was all that God could possibly ask for. So the life of Jesus reveals to us the meaning of the divine law in its most profound sense. As a result, living in union with the Son of God and striving to follow his example are the essentials of Christian morality.

"It is no longer I who live, but it is Christ who lives in me." Not only was Paul's mission given by Christ, his whole way of life was modeled on that of Jesus. This should be true, says Paul, not only of himself but also of all Chris-

tians. They too have *"clothed"* themselves with Christ and are *"one in Christ Jesus"* (Gal 3:27–28). In opposition to those who sought unity through obedience to commandments, Paul considers the Christian community to be an organic whole because of its union with Christ.

Paul's imitation of Jesus was so complete that he could even claim in the conclusion of the Letter to the Galatians that he bore the marks of Jesus on his body (6:17). This does not necessarily mean that he bore the wounds in a literal sense, as some mystics have. He simply may be referring to his sufferings on behalf of the gospel. Just as in Paul's time the branding of animals was a sign of ownership, he feels that because he has endured so much for the sake of Christ he belongs completely to the Lord.

Experience and Tradition

Paul's influence on the development of Christianity, the impact of his personality on the other members of the young community, and the dynamic energy he displayed in spreading the gospel may lead us to the conclusion that he almost single-handedly built up the Christian church. However, such a conclusion would not be true.

Christianity was already up and running by the time Paul arrived on the scene. The main centers of the faith—Jerusalem, Antioch, and Rome—were already evangelized when he put pen to paper. As indicated above, Paul needed the right hand of fellowship from Peter and the other apostles to give his work the stamp of authenticity. Though he may have grumbled about the "so-called pillars," he realized his own mission needed their approval.

In the creeds, liturgical formulae, and hymns sprinkled throughout his Letters, Paul used material in circulation when he became a follower of Christ. He too received instruction in the basic tenets of Christian doctrine: *"For I handed on to you as of first importance what I in turn had received: that Christ died for our sins in accordance with the scriptures, and that he was buried, and that he was raised on the third day in accordance with the scriptures, and that he appeared to Cephas, then to the twelve"* (1 Cor 15:3–5).

This concise statement of faith in the resurrection of Jesus is probably one of the earliest creeds. In dealing with the denial of Christ's resurrection by members of the Corinthian church, Paul first recites a creed already in vogue, and then refers to his own experience. After appearing to many others, the Lord appeared to him as *"to one untimely born"* (15:8).

Paul's teaching too was subject to the rule of faith. Whatever he knew about Jesus, apart from the doctrine of the resurrection, would have been told to him by other Christians. His knowledge of the "Abba" prayer of Jesus, for example, was certainly passed on to him by the first disciples. In addition to the resurrection creed, Paul uses other short professions such as Romans 4:25 (Jesus our Lord *"was handed over to death for our trespasses and was raised for our justification"*).

The same holds true for the reference to the celebration of the Lord's Supper in 1 Corinthians 11:23–26. The Eucharist was part of the tradition he received and which he in turn passed on to his converts. Consequently attempts to project Paul as the supreme improviser, the person who brought order into the "creative mass" of early Christianity, is to forget just how much had been achieved before he came on the scene.[4]

Paul's denial that his gospel was of human origin or that he was taught by anything other than a revelation of Jesus Christ (Gal 1:11–12) has to be put in context. As the background of the Letter to the Galatians reveals, Paul was rebutting the charge that his commission was not in the same class as that of the "pillar apostles." To counter such assertions he stressed his dependence on divine revelation.

This claim could hardly mean that he learned all he knew of the faith directly from one mysterious encounter with the resurrected Christ. Paul himself speaks of his experience as nothing more than a vision; there is no indication of heavenly messages or words being spoken in his

Letters. We also have to bear in mind his clear declaration that he too has received the creed that he is handing on to others.

Even though the major themes of Paul's teaching are phrased differently than the Gospel writers, the underlying beliefs are the same. He speaks of the suffering and death of Jesus. He stresses the significance of Christ's resurrection and calls attention to the Lord's coming in glory at the end of time. Paul's doctrines already outline the main elements of the story that will be told at greater length and detail in the four Gospels.

Paul's denial of any knowledge of Jesus *"from a human point of view"* (2 Cor 5:16) has been interpreted in various ways. The most likely explanation is that before his conversion Paul had a limited ("human") way of looking at Christ. He now sees Christ with the eyes of faith. Belief in the resurrection gives Paul a new perspective on the significance of Jesus. This vision is the basis of his ministry.

Though he did accept much from those who preceded him in the faith, Paul also represents a significant development in the history of Christianity: He did not just repeat parrot-fashion the teachings in which he has been instructed. In his missionary activity he faced fresh situations and challenges. He sought to make the Christian message relevant to the people he was leading in the faith. A new formulation of doctrine was required to allow the message of Jesus to flourish in very different environments.

After the world mission had gotten under way, a development that was not due to his initiative, Paul's energy and intellectual powers were able to carry forward this great movement. The Christian community was now finding its way through uncharted waters and Paul concentrated on the issues that needed immediate attention.

The death and resurrection were the supremely important facts about Jesus for Paul. Everything else was secondary by comparison. The resurrection of Jesus from the dead was the event that most deeply impinged on Paul's consciousness. Through his personal encounter with the risen Christ, Paul could sum up his faith in one resounding cry: "Jesus is Lord."

The hymn to Christ the Lord, which Paul inserts into his Letter to the Philippians (2:6–11), is the supreme expression of his faith. What adds to the significance of this hymn is the likelihood that Paul borrowed it from an earlier Christian source. So this meditation on the mystery of Christ comes from the first generation of disciples. Its theme is similar to what is found in the fourth Gospel (John), written so much later (possibly in the early second century).

Paul inserted into his Letter to the Philippians a contemporary Christian hymn to Jesus that spoke of his divine nature, the humiliation of his incarnation, and the even greater humiliation of his death. The hymn goes on to describe his exaltation in heaven, the adoration of him by the universe, and the new name of Jesus: "Lord." Thus this early canticle praises the glorious name that Paul uses for the risen Christ, "Lord," and gives poetic utterance to the Christian practice of worshiping Jesus.[5]

When Paul calls Jesus the Lord he is declaring the dominion of Christ over the world and all history. The title does not refer to Jesus in his earthly condition, nor even to his role as judge at the end of time, but rather to his status as the Risen One. In his risen glory, Jesus the Lord is an influence vitally affecting the lives of his followers.

Christ now reigns majestically as the Lord of the living and the dead. At the same time, the hymn recalls the humble example of the historical Jesus. Though he was in the form of God from the beginning, he did not cling to his status but, through his submission even to death on a cross, he has become the pattern of conduct for the disciples of all ages.

Reflections

There have been many attempts in modern times to formulate the focal point of Paul's experience. However, in trying to locate this center we are faced with the difficulty that

Paul's Letters, with the exception of Romans, are occasional, unsystematic, and respond to particular problems. They presume a basic doctrine already given in the initial instruction. The material at our disposal does not give us a fully rounded insight into Paul's practice of the Christian faith.

The problem of knowing the mind of Paul is illustrated by the fact that we are told his eucharistic teaching only because the community at Corinth raised a specific question on this issue. Otherwise we might think that the Eucharist did not feature in his life at all.

Again with the exception of Romans, Paul's Letters deal with questions raised by his converts. He addresses the particular difficulties that have arisen after introducing them to the faith. This variety of issues and concerns accounts for the fragmentary nature of his reflections. At the same time, the spontaneous tone of his Letters gives them their directness and appeal to the modern reader. Paul is always ready to advise, enlighten, and admonish. He shares his own experience of the mystery of Christ as he grapples with the issues confronting the Christian community in a variety of new cultures.

Everything flows from his encounter with the risen Lord. His writing is the application to concrete circumstances of his conversion, the working out of his own experience. Paul's Letters are the transition from a personal awareness of Christ to the religious language in which that awareness is expressed.

The classical Protestant view has been that the core of Paul's preaching is justification by faith: He felt he had been saved and made righteous in the sight of God only through faith in his Son. This is seen as the central teaching of the Letter to the Romans which, together with Galatians, has remained, since the time of Martin Luther, the key statement of Protestant faith. However, in recent years there has been a move away from this position.[6]

The traditional Catholic opinion puts great emphasis on Paul's insight into the incarnation, the assumption of a human nature by the divine Son.[7] This too has been criticized as too static a view because the incarnation was seen by Paul as but the (necessary) step to the saving event of the cross: the passion, death, and exultation of the Son of God.

Many commentators, both Protestant and Catholic, accept that the simplest summary of Paul's vision of Christianity is the phrase "in Christ," which occurs so frequently in his writings. The new relationship he entered as a result of his conversion is most pithily summed up in this expression. The phrase "in Christ" is Paul's most powerful way of describing his own life and his sense of union with the Lord.

The claim to be "in Christ" is a supremely personal statement. Paul's awareness of being united with the risen Lord also explains why he was not overly concerned with the details of the historical life of Jesus. Christ does not just stand before the Christian as a figure of history. He is, above all, the "life" of the faithful disciple.

For Paul, Jesus was not a person of the past, but a living life-giving Lord with whom he had a vital and dynamic relationship in the here and now. As a result, his spiritual life was one of action. His vision of the risen Lord was the beginning of a commitment to the gospel. He lived out that commitment in total self-giving as an apostle. He was immersed in the world of his day and traveled by land and sea, through towns and cities, seeking occasions to spread the good news and bring people to conversion.

Life "in Christ" is the clearest description of Paul's spirituality. This phrase sums up his Christian identity. Living "in Christ" most accurately describes the new life that began after his encounter on the road to Damascus.

Being "in Christ" means belonging to the person of Christ at the deepest level of one's being. No other expression of Paul captures so well the close union of the Christian with his heavenly Lord. Because of the depth of this mystical relationship, Paul could say on behalf of all followers of Jesus: *"It is no longer I who live, but it is Christ who lives in me"* (Gal 2:20).

TWO

Taking Up the Cross

The Way of Discipleship in Mark

"The greatest script I ever found" was how the actor Alex McCowen described Mark's Gospel. McCowen's one-man show consisted entirely of a reading of Mark, his only prop being a chair. The success of the performances brought out the character of Mark and highlighted the dramatic nature of the first Gospel. Mark gives us an action-packed, fast-moving story about a prophet and his confrontation with the world of his day.[1]

Mark's style greatly adds to the pace of the narrative. What has been called his breathless Greek comes over even in modern translations. The simplicity of the account makes Mark the ideal starting point for a reading of the New Testament. Indeed, the author has been criticized because of his limited vocabulary and his excessive use of such words as "immediately" and "then." However, if the evangelist lacks elegance, his vivid and direct speech enlivens the way he tells the story of Jesus.

The journalistic style of Mark's writing is deceptive and conceals his genius and the extent of his accomplishment. "Stark, dark, laconic Mark" has for long been considered the dunce among the evangelists. Yet he was not merely stringing stories together without any concern for the development of the plot. Nor was he just writing a passion narrative with a lengthy introduction, as a German scholar once dismissively described his Gospel.

The early tradition says that Mark wrote after the death of St. Peter in A.D. 64. On the basis of this, the date is usually set at somewhere between A.D. 65 and 70. That would make Mark the first Gospel.

Rome has generally been seen as the place where Mark was written. Many scholars accept this because of the connection with Peter who in the past was believed to have provided the Roman community with information about Jesus' words and actions. The teaching of Mark on the need of disciples to follow Jesus courageously would have had particular relevance for the Christian community in Rome during the persecution of Nero. However, Rome was not the only place where Christians endured persecution.

Mark's Gospel is the vital link in the New Testament. He drew the different sources circulating at the time into a connected story, thus preserving them for posterity in a solid, unified form. Using the accounts of miracles and sayings relating to the life and death of Jesus current in his day, Mark composed a story with a beginning, middle, and end. In doing so, he invented the genre that we now know as a Gospel. This has turned out to be the most appealing of all biblical forms.

In the past Mark was regarded as the most "historical" of the Gospels. It was considered to have given us the most accurate record of the life of Jesus. But we have to be wary of reading Mark as a historical account, in our modern sense. The Gospel writers were not primarily concerned with a precise report of what Jesus said and did. They used their sources freely to get the message across. The same is true of Mark. He tailored his material according to his own particular vision of Christ and his church.

The first Gospel is fundamentally a message for the Christian reader. The title is meant to alert us to the content of the story, *"the gospel about Jesus Christ, the Son of God."* His entire narrative, Mark states, will give a description of how the good news was first proclaimed. The focus of this narrative will be Jesus Christ. But the good news also contains a message about the cross. As the drama unfolds, Mark's Gospel reveals the mystery of the Son of God who is also the suffering Son of man.

To understand Jesus properly, warns Mark, the reader must see him not only as a preacher, a teacher, and a healer but, above all, as the Son of God who submits to crucifixion and whom his Father raises to glory. This is the message that Mark wants to convey. There can be no separation between the teaching of Jesus and who he claims to be. The fate of Jesus is intimately connected with his identity as the beloved Son of God.

The Twelve Disciples

Each of the Gospels looks at Jesus from a particular point of view. We shall consider how the other evangelists see him in the succeeding chapters. Mark portrays Jesus first and foremost as a teacher. Not only does Jesus set out to teach in this Gospel, his disciples and the religious leaders with whom he has contact address him as teacher.

Like Matthew and Luke, Mark contains extended sections of instruction. Jesus teaches, often in parables, and his words are confirmed by mighty deeds. The purpose of the miracles is to confirm the message. The teaching of Jesus gives the true meaning of the miracles.

The same divine power inspires both the teaching and the miracles. These two elements of Jesus' activity, his teaching and his miracles, are often combined, as happens after the cure of the possessed man in the synagogue: *"They were all amazed, and they kept on asking one another, 'What is this? A new teaching—with authority! He commands even the unclean spirits, and they obey him'"* (1:27).

Jesus comes across powerfully in the first Gospel as a mighty wonder worker. But he is not portrayed as a magician. The miracles back up the message he is teaching. Far from being automatically guaranteed, the miracles are closely connected with the faith of the witnesses and even depend on the faith of those who benefit from them.

Mark shows that miracles on their own do not necessarily lead to faith; they do not automatically produce a positive response. The Pharisees were unimpressed. After the cure of the man with the withered hand, far from being won over by such a gracious act of mercy, they started to conspire with the Herodians to kill Jesus (3:6). The scribes denounced the miracles of Jesus as the work of the devil (3:22). Therefore miracles on their own do not compel the observers to the obedience of faith.

Like all the great teachers of his day, Jesus had a band of close followers who were known as his disciples. They formed his circle. The impression we get from the Gospel is that Jesus had a large circle of disciples and they included both men and women. Mark 3:34–35 confirms this: *"And looking at those who sat around him, he said, 'Here are my mother and my brothers! Whoever does the will of God is my brother and sister and mother.'"*

The whole company of disciples was closely associated with Jesus. Yet within this larger grouping, twelve specially chosen disciples, also known as apostles, enjoyed a particular intimacy with their teacher. Mark stresses this association; the Twelve are the core group. In addition to serving as examples for later disciples, they have a role that goes beyond their own call and function. The Twelve represent the new Israel brought into being by the preaching of Jesus.

Mark first presents "the Twelve" in a very positive light. He does this in two closely linked scenes: The initial call of the disciples in chapter 1 and the final selection of the Twelve in chapter 3: *"As Jesus passed along the Sea of Galilee, he saw Simon and his brother Andrew casting a net into the sea—for they were fishermen. And Jesus said to them, 'Follow me and I will make you fish for people.' And immediately they left their nets and followed him. As he went a little farther, he saw James son of Zebedee and his brother John, who were in their boat mending the nets. Immediately he called them; and they left their father Zebedee in the boat with the hired men, and followed him"* (1:16–20).

Jesus begins his ministry by inviting particular people to follow him. Mark's opening chapter describes the call of these individual disciples and, at the same time, gives important instruction on discipleship. The response of the disciples conveys to the reader the authority and drawing power of the one who calls. There are no hesitations or delays.

Unlike John and Luke, Mark gives no indication that Simon and Andrew already know Jesus. This adds to the urgency of the summons and the immediacy of their reaction. By recounting the vocation of those early disciples in this way, Mark is reminding his community that Christians should obey Jesus' commands with courage and generosity.

The invitation to become "fishers of people" points out the meaning of the disciples' vocation and indicates the kind of training they will receive from Jesus. The image was not totally original. In describing his call, Jeremiah proclaimed the divine warning that God would employ fishers and hunters to catch the erring people and bring them for judgment (16:16). Jesus uses the image in a positive sense. There is no mention of judgment. The apostles will bring those they catch into the kingdom of God.

The invitation to come behind Jesus has a special significance. The Twelve must learn from his way of dealing with people if they are eventually to be sent forth as fishers. Living in the company of the master they will not undergo a process of abstract learning. The nature of their apprenticeship has a practical bent. The apostles are to be trained so that, like Jesus, they can go out to win men and women for the kingdom of God: *"And he appointed twelve, whom he also named apostles, to be with him, and to be sent out to proclaim the message, and to have authority to cast out demons"* (3:14–15).

In the appointment of the Twelve a final selection of the central group of disciples is made. Mark now knits the four mentioned in the first chapter into a symbolic pattern of twelve. Like the twelve sons of Jacob, these disciples represent the twelve tribes called into being to renew the people of Israel.

The evangelist puts the stress on the action of Jesus. He *made* twelve, according to the original Greek text. Unlike the teachers of his day who accepted disciples who wanted to learn, Jesus picks out those whom he wishes to instruct in the mysteries of the kingdom. He gathers a small group of intimates to share his life and be the privileged recipients of the explanations concerning his identity and mission.

The Twelve are called to be "with Jesus." Their training consists of watching him, hearing him, and following his example. Even if they are not the only ones in the circle of disciples, Mark portrays the Twelve as the most important figures. They occupy the center of the picture throughout the Gospel. Once the Twelve are appointed they remain constantly at Jesus' side.

The only interruption of this association occurs in chapter 6 when the Twelve are sent out on mission and, significantly at that point in the narrative, Mark switches from the activity of Jesus to speak about the fate of John the Baptist. Jesus and the Twelve have become inseparably bound together. Through his description of the close relationship of the disciples to Jesus, Mark is calling the followers of Christ in succeeding generations to stand in a similar intimate communion with their divine Lord.

The purpose of the disciples' call is a double one. Preaching and casting out devils are closely linked together. Because teaching and exorcism in the ministry of Jesus are directly linked to each other, those who are to continue his work must be trained to carry out the same dual task. Right at the beginning of their calling, the disciples are given an indication of what their future mission will entail. The good news they preach about the Son of God will also involve continuing his activity as a teacher and exorcist. In this way they will be true ambassadors, real apostles, of Jesus Christ.

So skill in teaching is not sufficient. This has to be combined with the power to cast out the forces of evil. Jesus' attack on the dominion of Satan is an important feature of the Marcan story. The power to cast out demons is an essential endowment of the Twelve as they continue the work of their master. Mark does not hide the fact that the major obstacle to the fruitful preaching of the gospel is the opposition of the devil.

Right from the early stages of his ministry, Jesus is caught up in a struggle with the demons. His mission is to destroy the stranglehold of Satan and to do this he has to engage directly with the diabolical powers. Mark even goes so far as to say that Jesus was driven by the Spirit into the desert to be tempted by Satan for forty days.

The opposition of the evil one to the preaching of Jesus is continued in the lives of the disciples. But Jesus gives them confidence and makes clear where the ultimate victory will lie. The parable of the strong man plundering the goods of his adversary (3:22–30) alludes to the victory of Jesus over the devil and assures his disciples that Satan will not have the power to destroy their work.

Chapter 3 describes both the final selection of the Twelve and the beginning of the conflict between Jesus and his opponents. The central action of the story begins at this point. After the cure of the man with the withered hand, the Pharisees and the Herodians plot together to kill Jesus (3:6). This is a decisive moment in Mark's drama.

The scheming between those who were traditionally rivals for power indicates that the final rupture between Jesus and the religious leaders of Israel is already a foregone conclusion. As a consequence, Jesus will focus his attention on the Twelve: *"To you has been given the secret of the kingdom of God, but for those outside, everything comes in parables"* (4:11).

The Twelve will be endowed with all the necessary gifts to ensure the effectiveness of their mission. The Twelve are called "apostles" ("those sent out") for the first time in 6:30. The familiar title "twelve apostles" has its origin here. The initial foray described in chapter 6, however temporary it may have been, already gives a foretaste of the universal mission.

The Way of Discipleship

Mark's narrative has been called the Gospel of "the Way." The central part (8:27–10:52) takes the form of a journey that begins far from Jerusalem at Caesarea Philippi and ends at Jericho, the town nearest to Jerusalem. But the journey is not just a geographical passage; it is also an inner process of faith. As the Twelve accompany Jesus on the road, he reveals to them what following him entails. The hard realities of discipleship are not minimized; but they are always related to the hope of resurrection.

Mark is giving a warning to his fellow Christians on the implications of their commitment. At the same time, he shows how the light of God shines through the life of Jesus and leads those who come after him along the road to glory.

The manner in which Mark made this journey central to his story sets a trend that was followed by other New Testament writers. In Luke's Gospel there is a long section dealing with the journey of Jesus to Jerusalem. The Acts of the Apostles describes Christians as the people of "the Way." In the fourth Gospel Jesus refers to himself as "the Way" and the Letter to the Hebrews describes the pilgrimage of the people of God.

The first evangelist presents his teaching on discipleship within a living framework. He describes the actual process by which the Twelve are summoned to enter a deeper knowledge of their master. Like their forebears in the Old Testament, these first followers of Jesus are painted as thoroughly human. Along the way we have a dramatic insight into their fears, their search for earthly glory, and their hardness of heart.

Jesus starts his journey to Jerusalem with a question that sets the tone for everything that follows: *"On the way he asked his disciples, 'Who do people say that I am?'"* (8:27). Only in the correct response to this question can the disciple understand what following Christ involves.

Jesus will answer the question himself through the encounters and incidents that occur along the road from

Galilee to Jerusalem. The journey will reach a climax with the cure of the blind beggar as Jesus enters Jericho. Bartimaeus will receive the gift of sight and become a follower of Jesus. By concluding the long section of instruction on the Way with a cure of physical blindness, Mark makes his point: Those who listen with open hearts to the teaching of Jesus will be cured of spiritual blindness. They will be able to see the way forward and be empowered to follow the Son of God.

Three predictions of the passion are given on the way to Jerusalem. Through the triple reference to the coming suffering, Mark keeps clearly before the mind of the reader that Jesus cannot be understood apart from his passion and death. These painful events are a necessary part of God's plan and cannot be avoided if he is to remain faithful to his mission. At the same time the sufferings of Jesus are never isolated from the promise of resurrection.

The First Prediction of the Passion

In reply to the question about the identity of Jesus, Peter makes a confession of faith. As distinct from other people's perceptions, Peter, on behalf of all the disciples, proclaims that Jesus is the Messiah. This act of faith is an important moment in the Gospel. Peter shows how far the disciples have progressed in their understanding of Jesus. The declaration that Jesus is the Christ, the anointed one of God, sums up the revelation that has been given to them in the first part of the Gospel. However, in what immediately follows we see how incomplete is the understanding of Peter and the rest of the Twelve.

The confession of Peter is followed by the first prediction of the passion: *"Then he began to teach them that the Son of Man must undergo great suffering, and be rejected by the elders, the chief priests, and the scribes, and be killed, and after three days rise again"* (8:31).

While in no way denying the truth of Peter's confession, Jesus is quick to clarify the implications of the pronouncement. He warns his disciples that the Messiah will not be a king of glory. Rather he must follow the way of the suffering Son of man. Right away human expectations are shaken and those who would follow Jesus are brought up short with the reality of Christian discipleship. Here we have the essence of the teaching on the Way. Jesus "must" suffer and be put to death.

Yet we have to be careful how we interpret this "must." Jesus will be rejected and put to death, not because of the implacable anger of God, but because of the implacable hostility of his enemies. If these enemies pursue their intention to kill him, Jesus must still be faithful to his Father's will. He must carry out his mission even if this means the sacrifice of his life. Nobody can be allowed to deflect Jesus from the divine purpose.

Hence Jesus' stunning response to Peter's advice to run away from the cross: *"Get behind me, Satan!"* (8:33). These words have often been misunderstood. Jesus is not telling Peter to go away and cease being a disciple. On the contrary, he is calling Peter back to the attitude he had when he was first called. Then he was told to fall in "behind Jesus," and walk in the footsteps of his master. Now a similar order is given. Though this interpretation gives Jesus' command a more positive sense, the force of the reprimand is not lessened. Jesus "rebuked" Peter in the same way he "rebuked" the evil spirit who possessed the man in the synagogue in an earlier incident (1:25).

Peter's resistance to the destiny of Jesus is implicitly a refusal to accept such a possibility for himself. His reaction to the first prediction of the passion shows that he too is possessed by an evil spirit. He has become a tempter, like Satan, to Jesus. The result of this diabolical influence is the fact that Peter has set his mind on "human things" rather than "the things of God." The only way he can be delivered from such a malign influence is to stay close behind Jesus and thereby maintain his attitude of faithful commitment.

Peter is not alone in his false reaction. The resistance of the other disciples to "the things of God" starts to build up and will come to a head in Jerusalem. Despite the efforts of Jesus to enlighten them, the disciples do not properly grasp the nature of their call. They will not be able to comprehend the meaning of the suffering of Jesus or accept the implications of this suffering for themselves. Their failure will be the outcome of vain ambition and hardness of heart.

So this central section of the Gospel not only gives a warning of the coming passion but also explains the reasons why the disciples failed to hold fast when the storm broke upon them. The cause of their infidelity is summed up in the words of Jesus: They did not hold dearly "the things of God." *"He called the crowd with his disciples, and said to them, 'If any want to become my followers, let them deny themselves and take up their cross and follow me'"* (8:34). These words are not a call but rather a clarification of the call. The explanation is not addressed specifically to the disciples, but to the people at large. The pronouncement is directed to the reader as well. The invitation is therefore given to all and the conditions of following Christ are made clear.

Discipleship is defined as a taking up of the cross and falling in behind Jesus. The command indicates the need for constancy on the part of the Christian. A burst of initial fervor is not enough. By accepting the reality of the cross from the beginning, the disciples acknowledge what they are facing as they walk along the Way. They must brace themselves for the persecution that will come upon them. Yet they are safe if they keep "behind Jesus." Fixing their eyes on him they will be drawn along by the power of the Son of God.

The first prediction of the passion is followed by the transfiguration of Jesus on the mountain in the presence of Moses, Elijah, and three disciples (9:2–13). The words of the Father are important because both the vision and the voice have a part to play in identifying Jesus. The scene is another way of responding to the question posed at the beginning of the journey about who he is.

The transfiguration is a revelation that Jesus is the beloved Son of God. The message given at the baptism in the first chapter is repeated. Yet here again, although there is a clear revelation, the three disciples who are present fail to understand the meaning of the vision and the words. The revelation of the glory of Jesus, like the prediction of the passion, is met with incomprehension.

Peter's offer to build three tents is evidence that he is confused by what he sees and hears. His desire to prolong the effects of the experience is judged negatively by the narrator: He *"did not know what to say, for they were terrified"*(9:6). In Mark's Gospel fear is always a negative reaction to the mighty deeds of Jesus. Fear is the opposite of a faith-filled response. Even though only Peter's reaction is described, the reader is left to understand that he is acting here as a spokesman for the other disciples, just as he was when he confessed Jesus as the Messiah.

After the descent from the mountain, the failure of the disciples to perform an exorcism is a further indication to the reader of their weakening faith. They had previously been sent to cast out evil spirits and had successfully performed their task (6:13). Now they are incapable of curing a mere boy. This lack of faith draws an angry response from Jesus: *"How much longer must I be among you? How much longer must I put up with you?"* (9:19).

The Second Prediction of the Passion

Mark's second prediction of the passion introduces a further consideration of the refusal of the Twelve to accept the terms of discipleship (9:30–10:31). It consists of a number of incidents carefully selected and put together by the evangelist to deepen our awareness of that way of thinking that will always pose a threat to fidelity. In particular, Mark illustrates three dispositions that will undermine discipleship or even render a person incapable of accepting the call in the first place—preoccupation with status and power, unchaste living, and attachment to riches.

Pride is a major obstacle to following Jesus on the way to suffering and rejection. The failure of the Twelve is rooted in their desire to be considered important members of the community. With supreme irony, the evangelist indicates how the warning of Jesus has not penetrated the hearts of the disciples. He has said he must lay down his life. In their obtuseness, the Twelve immediately get embroiled in an argument about which of them is the greatest.

To counteract this attitude, Jesus plays out a living parable by bringing a child into their circle. He identifies himself with the weakest and the most humble members of society: *"Whoever welcomes one such child in my name welcomes me; and whoever welcomes me welcomes not me but the one who sent me"* (9:37).

However, individual members of the community are not the only ones who can become arrogant. The community as a whole, by developing an attitude of superiority to the rest of society, can be blind to the greatness found among those who are not formally disciples. To counteract such a tendency, Jesus points out that those who are not against us are for us. The good deeds of those outside the community will reveal where they really stand.

Following the warning against pride, Mark puts together three sayings about purity that leave the reader in no doubt about the necessity of a chaste life. Far better to lose an eye, a foot, or a hand than to be thrown into Gehenna (hell) *"where their worm never dies, and the fire is never quenched"* (9:48). The threat of final loss through being cast into hell shows that although Jesus is not forcing people to follow him, unwillingness to do so because of immoral practices will expose a person to a far greater loss.

The exhortation to chaste living leads into Jesus' teaching on divorce (10:1–12). The prohibition against divorce is first given to the Pharisees and the crowd, which includes the disciples, and finishes with a repetition to the disciples alone. The double ban underlines the importance of what Jesus has to say about an issue that was no doubt causing serious problems for the Christian readers of the Roman world.

The fact that the Pharisees ask the question in the first place is a reminder of the debate that was taking place in Judaism about divorce.[2] As a teacher new to the scene, Jesus is tested about his view on the matter. He presents his revocation of the divorce concession as a revelation of the deeper meaning of the commandments. The disciples must seek the will of God with a generous heart and not look for dispensations.

The Twelve ask Jesus for further clarification on the issue when they go indoors. He reinforces what he has already said and takes the argument to its logical conclusion: *"Whoever divorces his wife and marries another commits adultery against her"* (10:11). Here too the radical nature of Jesus' demands is evident and he displays his authority to change the accepted customs of the day. In the Jewish legal system of the time, adultery could only be committed against a husband; women did not have the same protection under the law.

The third major obstacle to following Jesus is attachment to riches. This point is made in the story of the man who refuses the call (10:17–25). Together with the words about wealth and the promise of a reward to the faithful disciple, the episode puts before the reader further consequences of coming after the Son of man.

The dialogue between Jesus and the prospective follower (Matthew adds to the drama of the encounter by describing him as young) defines the cost of discipleship. External observance of the commandments is not enough. Even though the man has kept them from his boyhood days, he experiences an inadequacy in his life. *"Jesus, looking at him, loved him"* (10:21). But he did not spare him in what was required. He was told he must give away all he possesses to the poor, and then walk behind Jesus.

Although the earlier calls to leave everything seemed to present no problems, Mark now shows us that there is another possible response. Even when given with loving affection, the invitation of Jesus can be refused. Acceptance is a work of grace. Rejection can be traced to some human weakness. In this case we are told that the great wealth of the man caused him to turn away sadly. The reaction too is poignant: *"Jesus looked around and said to his disciples. 'How hard it will be for those who have wealth to enter the kingdom of God!'"* (10:23).

Peter's query about the fate of those who have taken up the invitation to leave everything and follow Jesus prompts a fitting conclusion to the teaching on the dangers of wealth: *"Truly I tell you, there is no one who has left house or brothers or sisters or mother or father or children or fields, for my sake and for the sake of the good news, who will not receive a hundredfold now in this age—houses, brothers and sisters, mothers and children, and fields with persecutions—and in the age to come eternal life"* (10:29–30).

The early Christian readers of Mark would have felt that the promise of recompense had a word of special comfort for them if they were undergoing the persecution mentioned rather awkwardly in the text.

The Third Prediction of the Passion

"They were on the road, going up to Jerusalem, and Jesus was walking ahead of them; they were amazed, and those who followed were afraid" (10:32). The moving detail that Jesus was walking ahead of them indicates the separation building up between him and the disciples. Later at the tomb the angel will tell them that Jesus will go before them to Galilee. This holds out the promise that eventually the disciples will be reunited with Jesus after the resurrection. But first they must follow him to the cross. The way they are holding back shows that they are incapable of such fidelity at the moment. Jesus and the whole company were distressed; those who followed him, the disciples, were afraid.

As they come close to Jerusalem the narrator makes it clear that far from having grasped the nature of the teaching on discipleship, the Twelve have remained uncomprehending. They are not only lacking in understanding but are even afraid to ask for explanations. In the earlier part of the Gospel the disciples had already given indications that they were not in tune with the thinking of Jesus. Now their resistance is about to lead them into disloyalty:

> See we are going up to Jerusalem, and the Son of Man will be handed over to the chief priests and the scribes, and they will condemn him to death; then they will hand him over to the Gentiles; they will mock him, and spit upon him, and flog him, and kill him; and after three days he will rise again. (10: 33–34)

To heighten the sense of foreboding and the approaching climax of the passion, the third prediction gives more details of the coming sufferings of Jesus. Yet again there is mention of the resurrection. The Gospel is good news, not a tragic tale, and the evangelist never wants the reader to see the passion of Jesus in isolation from its final outcome. The way of Jesus passes from death to resurrection. Those who walk behind him must keep their vision fixed on the victorious Leader who goes before them.

The third prediction is followed by another dispute about greatness among the disciples. Once more Mark asks his readers to reflect on the nature of their call and to be aware of the attitudes that can bring about a failure to respond faithfully. The dispute about greatness highlights the incomprehension of the Twelve. James and John pinpoint the attitude of the whole group by seeing the journey to Jerusalem as a path to earthly glory and power. The others indignantly criticize the request of the two brothers for the places of greatest honor (which Matthew will later soften to the request of their mother). The vehemence of their protest is perhaps a sign that the brothers had stolen a march on them.

Mark 10: 42–45 gives us Jesus' final instruction "on the way." The pattern of prediction, incomprehension, and instruction is brought to a conclusion. There is one last effort to explain the meaning of true discipleship. While pagan rulers seek to exercise domination over others, the followers of Jesus must imitate the example of their teacher. He walks the path of service, humility, and obedience to God's will. Jesus explains for the first time the significance of his coming suffering and death: *"For the Son of Man came not to be served but to serve, and to give his life a ransom for many."*

This declaration captures the whole program of Mark's Gospel. The result of Jesus' self- sacrifice is the "ransom of many," that is to say, the liberation of those who are enslaved by the domination of evil. The authenticity of those who follow Jesus is decided by their willingness to dedicate themselves to the welfare of the community.

The concluding episode of the journey exemplifies the power of Jesus to liberate the hearts of his disciples. He has struggled with the Twelve all the way from the northern region of Caesarea Philippi almost down to Jerusalem. Now he performs a final healing miracle by curing the blind beggar Bartimaeus in Jericho (10:46–52).

Standing in contrast as it does to the blindness of the disciples, the restoration of the beggar's sight symbolizes the ability of Jesus to bring full vision to those who, like Bartimaeus, approach him with faith. The miracle is therefore an appropriate conclusion to the journey and to the teaching of Jesus on the way of discipleship. To strengthen the impact of his conclusion, Mark tells us that Bartimaeus was not only the recipient of a healing miracle but also joined the disciples of Jesus and followed him "on the way."

Mark's description of Jesus' journey from Galilee to Jerusalem has to be reckoned as one of the outstanding pieces of writing in the New Testament. The narrative moves quickly and contains both action and a deep understanding of the people involved. Mark swiftly takes the reader from the high point of the Gospel, the confession of Peter, through a series of revealing encounters to the arrival of Jesus at Jericho and the symbolic miracle of the blind man's cure.

While Jesus moves forward to his destiny with determination, the Twelve begin to hang back and become increasingly weak in their commitment. As Jesus spells out the obligations of discipleship along the way, the Twelve distance themselves both physically and spiritually from his demands. An ever-widening gap emerges between Jesus and his followers.

Mark is preparing the reader for the complete failure of the disciples during the passion. We are left in no doubt that the flight and betrayal of the Twelve were not the sudden, unexpected reactions of men overcome with fright. They were the inevitable result of their resistance to the teaching of Jesus on the way of discipleship.

The Mission of the Disciples

The disciples enter Jerusalem in triumph with Jesus. The victory, however, is illusory. Soon the superficiality of the crowd is brutally revealed. As events unfold, the loyalty of the Twelve is undermined and Jesus is betrayed, denied, and abandoned. The self-love of the disciples and their inability to think "the things of God" lead them into defection. Hardness of heart has subverted their initial enthusiasm.

But this flight is not the end. Mark points to a reconciliation between Jesus and his twelve disciples after the resurrection. Just as he warns them about their coming apostasy, Jesus also makes them a promise: *"But after I am raised up, I will go before you to Galilee"* (14:28). Because Mark has already amply demonstrated the efficacy of Jesus' words, the reader can be in no doubt that this promise will be fulfilled.[3]

Right from the Gospel's beginning the disciples are prepared for a mission. The opening chapter points to future evangelical outreach when the twelve disciples set out to follow Jesus. Like the prophet Elisha when called by Elijah, they have to make a break with their families and occupations. Their new and more pressing role will be to gather together the community of the faithful in preparation for the judgment that is to come upon the earth. The urgency of this task demands total dedication. So they must leave everything to follow Jesus.

The Twelve will be fishers of people. This means that they are not to retreat into the desert like the followers of John the Baptist. On the contrary, they have a mission that will ultimately extend to the furthest corners of the earth.

The disciples are called to be "sowers of seed." Unlike the metaphor of fishing, which is not interpreted within the Gospel, that of the sower is given a full explanation (4:10–20). The apostle spreads the Word abroad. But this task is not just the planting of the initial message. There is also need for instruction among those who receive the seed in order to nurture and strengthen them.

Galilee is the place where the disciples are told to regroup after the resurrection and from there they will eventually go out on their universal mission. The promise of Jesus before his passion is repeated in the command of the young man to the women at the tomb (16:7). The ministry of Jesus began in Galilee and most of his activity recounted in Mark takes place there. Galilee was the territory where Jesus had all his initial success, whereas Jerusalem was the place of confrontation and rejection. So when they return to the north to meet their resurrected Lord, the apostles will renew the early ministry of Jesus on an extended scale. Their mandate will have the same character as that of Jesus' mission but will take them to the ends of the earth.

There are two items in the concluding chapters of Mark that make the universal outlook of the author even more explicit: The parable of the vineyard and the discourse of Jesus on the end of the world.

The Parable of the Vineyard (12:1–12)

The vineyard is an ancient metaphor for the chosen people, as we see from Isaiah 5:1–7. Mark's parable of the vineyard describes God's dealings with Israel from the perspective of his Son, Jesus. The culmination of the story is the sending of the heir to collect the fruits of the vineyard. The murder of the heir by the tenants is a way of describing the crucifixion. The punishment of the original tenants means that they have lost their privileged position. The vineyard has been transferred to others.

Through the death and resurrection of Jesus the role of Israel as a light to the Gentiles has been transferred to the young Christian community. The disciples of Jesus must continue his ministry until the end of the world. Just as the parable speaks of the persecution of the prophets, so too the apostles must be prepared to suffer as they carry out the divine commission to preach the gospel.

In his three predictions of the passion Jesus had portrayed himself as one about to suffer. At the same time he warned his disciples that they would have to face similar treatment. Whenever he spoke of his own passion he also mentioned the sufferings of those who wished to follow him. The turmoil that will come upon the community is hinted at in the parable of the vineyard. The apostles will share the fate of the servants who were beaten, treated shamefully, and killed. The warning becomes more explicit as Jesus looks ahead to the future mission of the church in the final instruction of the Gospel.

The Discourse on the End of the World (13:9–13)

Chapter 13 has a significant place in Mark, coming as it does immediately before the passion and death of Jesus. The long speech that forms the chapter has a similar purpose to that of the Last Supper discourse in John. Speeches of great men at the end of their lives are part of the tradition the evangelists inherited and adapted from the Old Testament.

The final discourse in Mark 13:9–13 is a prediction of the events leading up to the second coming of Christ. It is a revelation of the future and uses vivid imagery to describe the judgment of God on the world. The part of the address that deals with the mission of the disciples is at the middle:

As for yourselves, beware; for they will hand you over to councils; and you will be beaten in synagogues; and you will stand before governors and kings because of me, as a testimony to them. And the good news must first be proclaimed to all nations. When they bring you to trial and hand you over, do not worry beforehand about what you are to say; but say whatever is given you at that time, for it is not you who speak, but the Holy Spirit. (13:9–11)

Jesus warns those who are listening to him to be on their guard. Not only must the disciples immediately addressed be on their guard, the exhortation is given to every succeeding generation of the church. The text carries a message on the demands of discipleship similar to what has already been said "on the way" from Galilee to Jerusalem. Jesus is the Son of man who suffers for the sake of the kingdom of God. His disciples likewise have to be prepared to take up their cross with him.

The discourse on the end of the world looks far beyond the death of the Messiah to the future generations of disciples and their mission. The gospel must be preached in every land before the new age can dawn. The universal mission is the vital task of the church in the time between the resurrection and the second coming. Thus the discourse presents preaching to all nations as a task that has a vital place in the plan of God.

Mark was telling his fellow Christians that suffering was part of their missionary activity. Arrest and trial gave them the opportunity to proclaim their faith. But an even more significant contribution to the success of the early church was the presence of the Holy Spirit. Though more fully developed by the fourth evangelist (John) with the image of the Paraclete, the role of the Spirit in missionary animation is already present in Mark's Gospel. The Spirit will assist the followers of Jesus both in the steadfastness of their faith and the convincing witness of their beliefs.

Reflections

The disciples play a key role in the Gospel of Mark. The evangelist pinpoints their place right from the start. The relationship of the Twelve with the one who has called them to be "fishers of people" is a central issue in the Gospel. This relationship is an ever-changing reality and we can detect three significant stages in the process.

At the beginning of his public ministry Jesus calls the Twelve and makes them the core group of his disciples. Their initial response is generous. They are empowered by Jesus to preach, heal, and cast out evil spirits. At this early stage everything seems to proceed well and although there are some hints of problems to come, there is every reason to hope the story will continue to move along satisfactorily.

About halfway through the narrative the picture begins to change and the underlying negative attitudes of the disciples start to surface. The cause of the change is the teaching of Jesus on his forthcoming rejection and suffering. Preoccupied as they are with their own concerns and ambitions, the disciples fail or refuse to listen to what the master is telling them.

Despite Jesus' urging that they stay close behind and keep their eyes fixed on him, the disciples become afraid. Because they fail to comprehend what Jesus is saying about his mission, they are unable to grasp the implications of his teaching for their own lives. The root of this inability to respond is the fact that they are thinking "human things" and not "the things of God."

The widening gap between the Twelve and Jesus reaches a critical point in the passion. Here the disciples are revealed in all their weakness. Despite previous protestations of fidelity, the moment of testing finds them unprepared to follow the way of the cross. One betrays, one denies, and they all abandon Jesus. Though willing in spirit, they are shown to be severely weak in the flesh. Their all-too-human dispositions have undermined their loyalty and initial commitment.

But Mark leaves us with clear indications that the disastrous debacle of the passion is not the end of the story. Even when predicting his passion, Jesus has always associated it with resurrection. Furthermore he gives explicit instructions to the Twelve on a future reunion in Galilee. There at last they will be able to comprehend the full extent of the good news and be empowered to carry out the mission entrusted to them by the risen Lord.[4]

With the discourse on the end of the world and the events leading up to the final judgment, Mark leaves his readers in no doubt that the relationship of Jesus to his disciples is not over with the passing of the Twelve. It continues in the lives of the cross-bearing and faithful community of disciples down through the generations.

THREE

The Yoke of Christ

Discipleship and Law in Matthew

Mark's Gospel was written to stiffen Christian resistance in a time of persecution. Matthew faced a more complex situation. Though the Gospel of Mark was treasured and most likely given a prominent place in the liturgy of Matthew's church, the need was felt for a new presentation of the good news.

Scholars generally accept that Matthew wrote sometime around the middle of the 80s of the first century. If we accept this date, certain factors come to light. Most important of all, the first Jewish War had resulted in the destruction of the Jerusalem Temple in A.D. 70.

With the loss of this focal point, the Jewish authorities centered their attention on the synagogues and drew up new measures to regulate the services. The Pharisees intensified the codification of their legal traditions. Though it took a while for these reforms to be put into full effect, one immediate result was a ban on Christians from participating in Jewish worship. By the time Matthew came to write his Gospel all links with the local synagogue had been severed.

Thus Christianity was facing an unknown future as a predominantly Gentile community. The mission to the Jews had been, overall, a failure and the apostles realized that their best hope for the future rested with the large masses spread throughout the Roman Empire.

So Matthew was writing for a community that was rapidly changing from a predominantly Jewish Christian church to an increasingly Gentile one. At the same time the need to set down new roots was being impeded by internal problems. Along with the loss of the mother church in Jerusalem, the deaths of James, Peter, and Paul had left the community without its first dynamic leaders.

The Gospel of Matthew was therefore a pastoral attempt to meet the needs of the disciples in a time of transition to new forms of Christian life. Crucial to this pastoral response was the necessity of bolstering the moral authority of the church, now that it was cut adrift from its traditional base in Judaism. Without the support of the Mosaic law expounded in the synagogues, Christians had to find a way to deal with the moral issues raised by the pagans who were seeking admission into their ranks.

Disciples who had started out within a strict Jewish morality were facing new questions at the very time that they found themselves severed from the most vital ethical structures of Judaism. Law, then, and in particular the moral law, is a central concern in Matthew.[1] To deal with the crisis Matthew had at his disposal the Jewish traditions of his church. These were deeply imbedded in the Mosaic law but now needed to be transposed into another framework. The old wine had to be poured into new wineskins if it was to be safely preserved (9:17).

Matthew writes a new Gospel for a new time. This is clear when we compare him to Mark, the first evangelist. Mark's framework is used as the basis for a completely different building. Perhaps a better metaphor would be a new symphony, because Matthew's Gospel presents us with recurring motifs and themes rather than tightly separated compartments.

The basic story line remains that of Mark. Matthew reproduces 90% of the first Gospel, reshaping the material in his own way. He extends Mark's narrative at both ends;

he adds an infancy narrative to the beginning and develops the conclusion with a number of resurrection appearances. Into the body of the Gospel he weaves five elaborate discourses, each one dealing with some particular aspect of Christian teaching. The result is a magisterial presentation of the life and message of Jesus that has earned a place in the front rank of the Gospels.

Matthew is concerned above all with the moral response of the followers of Jesus. Besides developing their little faith (8:26), the disciples must profess their allegiance to Christ by the kind of lifestyle they lead. The radical nature of Christian discipleship lies in the fact that the followers of Jesus are called to be perfect as the heavenly Father is perfect (5:48).

Above all, their moral life is not merely a human self-control but is rooted in the presence of the risen Christ. The first covenant forged a bond between Yahweh and his chosen people. In the second covenant the church has a privileged relationship with the one whose name is Emmanuel, "God among us." Jesus' presence in the community is the starting point of Matthew's teaching on Christian discipleship.

The Presence of Christ

Matthew begins his Gospel by recounting the long line of forebears from whom Jesus was descended (1:12–18). He does this to connect the earthly presence of Christ with the flow of Israel's ancient history.

Throughout the Gospel there are constant references to the Old Testament. These point out how Jesus fulfills what had been promised to the chosen people. The life of Jesus is the decisive moment in history. Through his birth, passion, death, and resurrection Jesus has brought his people remission of their sins.

Matthew's vision extends from the revelation to Abraham and continues right down to the consummation of all human history. The opening scenes, which narrate the birth of Jesus, and the concluding vision of the risen Lord giving his final mandate to the apostles function as two brackets. They enclose continual references, in word and deed, to the divine presence of Emmanuel among his disciples.

Joseph rather than Mary occupies center stage in Matthew's account of the birth of Jesus. This is done to connect Jesus more clearly to the Davidic line, a birthright he received through the lineage of Joseph. The message of the angel to Joseph concludes with a reference to the prophecy from Isaiah. Here for the first time Matthew uses the familiar formula: *"All this took place to fulfill what had been spoken by the Lord through the prophet: 'Look, the virgin shall conceive and bear a son, and they shall name him Emmanuel,' which means, 'God is with us'"* (1:22–23).

The angel indicates the mission of the coming One by explaining the significance of his name. *Emmanuel* or "God-with-us" not only reveals who Jesus is but also points to his mission to reconcile the world with the Father. This first revelation of the divine name gives the reader a concise definition of the Messiah who has come to save his people from their sins. By putting the explanation at the beginning of the Gospel, Matthew shows that he is carefully working out his message on the presence of Christ in the church. Through the birth of "Emmanuel" God will come to dwell among his people. The essence of Matthew's Gospel is captured in this one name. Matthew's narrative is an elaborate working out of this insight into the personality of Jesus. Because of his origin, Jesus manifests the divine presence and can deliver the people from their sins.

Faithful to the way Mark has opened the public ministry, Matthew tells the reader that Jesus was empowered for his ministry with the divine Spirit. He proves himself perfectly obedient to his heavenly Father. He proclaims the gospel of the kingdom to the people of Israel and calls them to obedience. He preaches, teaches, and heals with divine authority.

To ensure the continuity of his life-giving presence in the world Jesus gathers together and trains a group of followers who will later be sent out to all the countries of the earth.

The Call of the Twelve

Matthew paints a more sympathetic picture of the Twelve than Mark. He underlines the bonds between them and their master. They are the privileged companions of Jesus. Although still capable of failure, the disciples are able in this Gospel to penetrate more deeply the mystery of Jesus' identity.

The call of various disciples is narrated in Matthew's Gospel. In each case the authentic response to the invitation of Jesus is the immediate relinquishing of everything. This reaction is set in motion by the attractive power of the one who calls. No preamble or justification is given; there is just a command to "come behind me" uttered by Jesus:

> As he walked by the Sea of Galilee, he saw two brothers, Simon who is called Peter, and Andrew his brother, casting a net into the sea—for they were fishermen. And he said to them, "Follow me, and I will make you fish for people." Immediately they left their nets and followed him. (Mt 4:18–20)

Jesus' directive is quite emphatic: "Follow me." The disciples who hear Jesus are expected to follow him, leaving behind their former way of life.

The gathering of the Twelve resembles the vocation of prophets like Samuel in the Old Testament. In the case of the disciples, however, the invitation to follow Jesus is personal. They follow him and learn from him in an intimate manner, not just through the observance of a written code. The disciples are not asked to come and study the law, as was the case with the rabbis of the day.

Jesus does not ask his disciples to withdraw from the world. They are not to form a monastic community like that of the Essenes, who left the world and retired into the desert. They are rather to remain in the world to "fish for people." In addition to a call to discipleship there is also a commission. These fishermen are to be sent out as apostles. They are to be the salt and light of society. As a witness to

Christ, their presence will be as conspicuous as a city built on the top of a hill.

Thus there is a double command: The disciples must leave everything and follow Jesus, yet they have to stay in the world to continue his mission and preach the coming of the kingdom of heaven. As the subsequent narrative shows, there is no total withdrawal from the ordinary tasks of life. The Twelve also continue to be fishers of fish!

The lifestyle of the disciples involves both separation and participation. This means that the followers of Jesus live in a certain tension between detachment from society because of their commitment to Christ and a continuing participation in the affairs of the world through their involvement in mission.

The radical nature of the disciple's vocation is clearly borne out by the injunction to leave the dead behind (8:21–22). Burying one's parents was one of the great obligations of Jewish law. In Roman culture also, refusal to do so would have been a grave act of impiety. As St. Augustine comments: "Only God can ask this." Nothing should prevent the disciple from accepting the call to follow behind Jesus.

The Great Commission

The final commission given in the last scene of Matthew sums up his Gospel and has been prepared for through the course of the narrative. The abiding presence of the risen Lord among his disciples was promised at the beginning. In the last of the great speeches, the so-called missionary discourse, the command to preach to all nations is given as a task to be completed before the end can come: "*And this good news of the kingdom will be proclaimed throughout the world, as a testimony to all the nations; and then the end will come*" (24:14). During the Last Supper Jesus renews the promise by telling the disciples that having risen from the dead he will precede them into Galilee (26:31–32). Now, after the resurrection, the great commission is finally given:

Then Jesus came to them and said, "All authority in heaven and on earth has been given to me. Go therefore and make disciples of all nations, baptizing them in the name of the Father and of the Son and of the Holy Spirit, and teaching them to obey everything I have commanded you. And remember, I am with you always, to the end of the age." (28:18–20)

The Acts of the Apostles also portrays the last resurrection appearance and ascension of Jesus on a mountain (1:6–12). But while Luke has Jesus departing from his disciples on the Mount of Olives, Matthew depicts Jesus coming to them on a mountain in Galilee. The different settings fit in perfectly with the vision of each author. Luke underlines the coming of the Holy Spirit after the departure of Christ; Matthew stresses the enduring presence of Jesus in the church and among his disciples.

Matthew links the authority of Jesus to his identity as the Son of God. This is seen especially in the way the evangelist constantly portrays him giving his teaching on mountains. Jesus is not just a Mosaic figure going up the mountain to receive the Word of God and pass it on to the people. He is the one who comes to the mountain to reveal the divine will to his disciples. Jesus makes the will of God manifest to the community of faith.

The risen Christ announces that the prophecy of Daniel 7:14 has been fulfilled: All the authority over creation promised to the Son of man has been given to him. So he can command a worldwide mission. Matthew had begun his Gospel by identifying Jesus as the Son of God. In his eyes, Jesus is the Son of God in a manner that can be attributed to no other human being. Now the exalted Son sends the apostles to preach his gospel to all nations and gives them the full assurance of heavenly support in their task.

"make disciples of all nations"

The limited mission to Israel that Jesus exercised during his public life is now extended to the whole earth. The revelation of Christ's majesty to the disciples entails a widening in their understanding of mission. They are no longer to go only to the lost sheep of Israel—the whole Gentile world will be the terrain of their endeavors.

Matthew emphasizes the Gentile mission in order to impress on his contemporaries the need to set their sights on the pagan world. The Jewish milieu in which they once lived has now, like the Temple, gone forever.

Already in the body of the Gospel, Matthew (at least indirectly) gives indications of the coming universal mission. Sages travel from far away to pay homage to the infant King. Jesus praises the faith of the pagan centurion (8:10). He yields to the pleading of the Canaanite woman and cures her daughter (15:28). Finally, in the parable of the wicked tenants, he warns the Jewish leaders that the kingdom of God will be taken away from them and given to a people who will produce its fruit (21:43).

The death and resurrection of Jesus mark the time when this change of direction takes place. On Calvary the Roman centurion and those with him, in contrast to the mocking priests and teachers of the law, make a great proclamation of faith: *"Truly this man was God's Son"* (27:54). This confession is a dramatic expression of the message that Matthew wants to give his community. In the lifetime of Jesus there were non-Jews who believed in him. Now, after his death, his followers should not be afraid to preach the gospel to the Gentiles and welcome them into the Christian faith.

"baptizing them in the name of the Father and of the Son and of the Holy Spirit"

Here we have a clear indication that on one central issue of the old order Matthew presents us with a rejection. The great commission dispenses with the rite of circumcision. The mandate of the risen Lord strikes at the very heart of the Old Testament practice. The repudiation of circumcision would have been totally unacceptable to rabbinical Judaism.

"teaching them to obey everything that I have commanded you"

The stress on teaching that has been a preoccupation of Matthew right through the public ministry is still maintained in the commission of the risen Christ. The apostles are to teach everything that Jesus has taught them. The central core of Matthew's Gospel is built around the five great speeches of Jesus. They cover a variety of issues and this is the teaching that the apostles are now commanded to pass on to others. The five discourses contain the bulk of the instruction that Jesus would have all disciples everywhere follow to the end of time.

Not one of the speeches is addressed to the religious leaders of the day. The audience Jesus addresses is composed primarily of his followers and the purpose of the discourses is to bring the lives of the disciples into conformity with his own example. The future disciples of Jesus are also, of course, the intended audience of these instructions. The Christian disciple in every generation is called "to be like his teacher" (10:25).

"And remember, I am with you always, to the end of the age"

The concluding pronouncement of the great commission forms a unity with the name of Jesus given in the first chapter of the Gospel: He is Emmanuel, God with us. We also have an echo of Jesus' promise to build up his church (16:18) and the pledge that he will be among his disciples whenever two or three gather in his name (18:20). So the assurance of the divine presence at the end of the Gospel is the final statement of Matthew's belief that the risen Lord is continuously at work in the Christian community.

"To make an end is to make a beginning. The end is where we start from." These lines of T. S. Eliot are appropriate here. The great commission given by the risen Son of God at the end of Matthew's Gospel is both an end and a beginning. It provides the key to understanding everything else and consists of the three elements, which are the basic themes running through the Gospel. First, Jesus solemnly declares that all authority over heaven and earth has been invested in him. Second, he is truly the Son of the living God. There follows the missionary command through which the Easter message will be proclaimed by the church to the furthest corners of the earth. Third, the apostles are promised that Christ will be present among them until the end of time.

The Yoke of Christ

The presence of Christ among his disciples has a specific purpose. He will assist them to carry the yoke that they take upon themselves when they decide to follow him and become his apostles.

The meaning of the yoke of Christ is spelled out in the central part of Matthew's Gospel when Jesus says:

> . . . All things have been handed over to me by my Father; and no one knows the Son except the Father, and no one knows the Father except the Son and anyone to whom the Son chooses to reveal him. Come to me, all you that are weary and are carrying heavy burdens, and I will give you rest. Take my yoke upon you, and learn from me; for I am gentle and humble in heart, and you will find rest for your souls. For my yoke is easy, and my burden is light. (11:27–30)

Before inviting disciples to come to him and take up his yoke, Jesus speaks about his relationship with God. These words are an important introduction. Jesus solemnly informs the disciples that no one knows the Father except the Son and those to whom the Son chooses to reveal him. His words, often referred to as "the cry of jubilation," are similar to the sayings of John's Gospel. There too Jesus says that no one knows God except the Son (John 1:18).

The disciples of Christ are those who have first been given an understanding of the kingdom. They are to be given an even deeper perception of the deeds and words of their teacher. Jesus will reveal to them the relationship that exists between himself and the Father.

"Come to me, all you that are weary and are carrying heavy burdens"

The command "come" occurs six times in Matthew. It is given at moments of decision. So, for example, Jesus calls the fishermen Peter and Andrew to come and follow him. A similar sense of urgency is found in the present text. Having thanked his Father for the revelation of hidden mysteries and described his own unique role in passing on this knowledge to others, Jesus urges his listeners to come to him. This too is a moment of decision. Those who are heavily burdened are invited to seek refuge in the presence of Christ. Coming to Jesus is the equivalent of the call to discipleship.

The word *burden* is used later in Matthew's Gospel to sum up the weight of legal interpretations constructed by the Pharisees. "So, in the present passage 'burden' should not be understood as a reference to sins or to the pressures of life. It is a reference to legal interpretation, similar to that in 23:4."[2] Those who feel burdened by the weight of the law are invited to leave their own teachers and come follow Jesus.

"I will give you rest"

The heart of Jesus' criticism of the Pharisees was their lack of solidarity with the people. It is not their legal position as such that angered him but their unwillingness to shoulder the burdens of the ordinary folk. Their isolation from the everyday difficulties showed they had forgotten the weightier matters of the law (23:23). The rest promised by Jesus is the assurance that he will enable his followers to bear the yoke that he will put upon them. "The rest promised by Jesus is not simply a reward to be granted only in the future. It is a gift for the present life—a correlative of the response to the invitation to discipleship."[3]

"Take my yoke upon you, and learn from me"

The yoke is the dominant figure of the double command that Jesus gives to those who want to become his disciples. This central image of the text is best understood from its background in the Old Testament. There the "yoke" was used to symbolize the law. Bearing this yoke was what made a person wise.

In the Book of Ecclesiasticus (Sirach), the young Israelite is urged to put his feet into the fetters of wisdom, his neck into her harness, and give his shoulder to her yoke (6:24–25). Later on the writer calls out:

> Draw near to me, you who are uneducated, and lodge in the house of instruction. Why do you say you are lacking in these things, and why do you endure such great thirst? I opened my mouth and said, "Acquire wisdom for yourselves without money. Put your neck under her yoke, and let your souls receive instruction; it is to be found close by." (51:23–26)

The author of Ecclesiasticus presents the acceptance of the yoke of wisdom as the way to happiness. This is even more clearly stated in chapter 24 with the promise that *"those who eat of me will hunger for more, and those who drink of me will thirst for more"* (v. 21). There is a clear parallel with the invitation of Jesus. He too offers his disciples the happiness that flows from a proper understanding of the law.

However, there is one significant difference between the words of Jesus and the literature of the Old Testament. In that tradition people were exhorted to submit to the yoke of wisdom. There is no instance of teachers referring to their own yoke. Teachers cannot speak of "their yoke" because obedience is due not to them but to the law.

In the minds of the rabbis contemporary to Jesus, accepting the yoke meant accepting the law. Discipleship was for the purpose of learning the law. Matthew, however, focuses on the person of Jesus. He is both wisdom itself and the sage who interprets wisdom. "So taking up the yoke of

Jesus becomes a correlative of discipleship, with that discipleship including 'obedience to the law as interpreted by Jesus' and an understanding of the mysteries of the Kingdom as disclosed by him."[4]

The word *yoke* instantly brings to mind the idea of a load or a burden. Used as an image for the law in Jewish thinking, the metaphor has a similar meaning in the teaching of Jesus. His yoke refers to the obligations that becoming a disciple entails.

The disciple is left in no doubt by the very force of the word *yoke* that becoming a follower of Jesus requires an active response. It involves responsibilities. The Christian has to take on board the moral content of Jesus' teaching, which is such a strong feature of Matthew's Gospel.

The kind of interpretation offered by Jesus is illustrated in the controversies over the Sabbath that follow the invitation to take up the yoke. The two Sabbath stories in 12:1–14 show how the yoke of Jesus differs from the rigorous interpretations of the scribes and Pharisees. In the defense of his disciples plucking the grains of wheat and in the cure of the man with the shriveled hand, Jesus applies the Sabbath law in a more merciful fashion than his opponents. Thus, accepting the yoke of Christ means rejecting the harsh authority of the Pharisees.

"Learn from me; for I am gentle and humble in heart"

These words of Jesus are a clear invitation to discipleship. To take up the yoke and learn from him are parallel expressions, which mean the acceptance of a closer union with him. He is the true teacher because he is meek and humble. The real disciple must imitate the attitude of the master as well as his instructions. Taking up his yoke, then, necessitates assuming the gentleness and humbleness of Jesus.

The scribes and Pharisees burdened their followers with rigorous interpretations of the law. Their inflexibility was quite the opposite of the gentleness and lowliness of

Jesus. This difference is pointed out again in the conclusion to the two Sabbath controversies in chapter 12. There Matthew applies the words of Isaiah to Jesus: *"He will not wrangle or cry aloud, nor will anyone hear his voice in the streets. He will not break a bruised reed or quench a smoldering wick . . ."* (12:19–20).

"You will find rest for your souls"

Jesus promises rest to those who take up his yoke. However, the combination of "yoke" and "rest" seems to be a contradiction. How can the yoke be easy and the burden light?

Matthew has given us a clue to the answer by associating the yoke of Jesus with discipleship. The yoke of Jesus is easy and his burden is light precisely because this yoke brings the disciple into communion with the One who is gentle and lowly of heart. Those who follow Jesus immediately enjoy peace of mind. The yoke of Jesus is light because of the presence of the One who offers it to the willing disciple.

Accepting the yoke of Jesus therefore means following Jesus and accepting his way of interpreting the law. Indeed, the phrase "the law of Christ," employed often to describe the moral instruction of Jesus, is another way of speaking of his yoke.

The Law of Christ

The relationship of the Christian to the moral law was a concrete problem faced on a daily basis in the early days of the community. Saint Paul himself had struggled with this question in his Letters to the Galatians and the Corinthians. The moral law was also one of Matthew's primary concerns.

The practical living out of Christian discipleship as perceived by Matthew is contained in the five great discourses that form the central spine of his narrative. In these sections of the Gospel, controversies between Jesus and the professional lawyers of his day abound. The "scribes and the Pharisees" are bitterly attacked by Jesus because of their legalistic interpretations.

Yet he does not question their task of interpreting the law. In one place he even enjoins obedience to their authority: *"The scribes and the Pharisees sit on Moses' seat; therefore, do whatever they teach you and follow it; but do not do as they do, for they do not practice what they teach"* (23:2–3).

In general, Matthew's attitude to the Jewish law was positive; this could hardly have been otherwise. The law of the Old Testament was not just a matter of ethical norms. It embraced the whole revealed Word of God. At a fundamental level, the "Law and the Prophets" remained the norm for Christian disciples also.

In describing the disputes between Jesus and the scribes, Matthew is using those controversies as a vehicle for putting across his own understanding of the law. His first aim is a pastoral emphasis on the necessity of keeping the deeper commandments, without getting entangled in the detailed observances proposed by the Jewish teachers.

The element of "fulfillment" shows the way in which Matthew deals with the Mosaic law. The prophecies and expectations of old are fulfilled in the person of Jesus. He has not come to destroy the law but to fulfill it (5:12). He brings the promises of the old covenant to their realization. At the heart of Matthew's teaching on the new law we find the person of Jesus.

Jesus requires allegiance not only to the basic principles of the covenant but above all to himself. His yoke is the one the disciple is obliged to carry. Matthew's faith in Jesus dominates everything else in the Gospel. He is truly Emmanuel, God with us. From this initial insight everything else proceeds, including the Christian interpretation of the law.

The new covenant replaces the Sinai covenant because the yoke of Jesus is the one the Christian takes up. The structure of the new covenant is built around Christ. In the old dispensation the individual belonged to the community through obedience to its laws. In the new order the disciple becomes a member of the church through allegiance to the Son of God. In both cases the moral order is lived out not in isolation, but within a community of faith and as a response to a divine initiative.

The Sermon on the Mount

The Sermon on the Mount is the first of the five great discourses that give Matthew's Gospel such a distinctive structure. Placed in an early and strategic position (chapters 5–7), the Sermon is the best indication we have of Matthew's attitude to the law. The very setting of the instruction, a mountain, immediately recalls the ascent of Moses to receive the tablets of the law on Sinai. If commentators can speak of "the Matthean range" because of the many mountain scenes described in this Gospel, the Sermon on the Mount presents us with Matthew's best known peak.

The mountain on which the Sermon is given points ahead to the mountain where the risen Lord will give his final command in the great commission. The teaching that the apostles are told to spread throughout the world is contained above all in this first major discourse.

The location of the Sermon on top of a mountain has prompted speculation that Jesus is being compared to Moses. The Book of Exodus speaks of Moses going up the mountain a number of times (19:3). When Jesus sits down on the top of the mountain he is assuming a posture of dignity. He proceeds to speak with great authority.

Another possible interpretation is that Jesus is presented as being far more important than Moses. He speaks in the place of God himself. The disciples who come up to listen to Jesus are those who stand in the place of Moses.

But whether we interpret Jesus as the new Moses or sitting in the place of God himself, there can be no doubt that the Sermon on the Mount is Matthew's presentation of the law of Christ. The new covenant, written on the heart according to Jeremiah 31:31–34, is now being given on the "holy hill" (v. 23). It is received by the people who joyfully gather "on the height of Zion" (v. 12). The expectation that the Messiah would bring about a renewal of the law is being fulfilled.

The disciples who go up the mountain with Jesus represent the community of those who have responded faithfully and now receive instruction on the requirements of their call. Matthew is naturally thinking of the Christians in his own community. "The real audience with which Matthew is concerned is not the four fishermen who have been called as disciples, nor the 'great crowds' which have come to him from all over the land, but the Christian believers of his own time; and the speaker is the risen Christ, who here makes his mind known to them on matters of lasting interest and importance in their lives and in the life of the church."[5]

The Beatitudes

The most original elements of the Sermon on the Mount are contained in the nine *beatitudes* that open the speech. They provide the unifying structure of the whole discourse and summarize what is essential to it. Consequently a word of explanation about what a beatitude means may be helpful.

The beatitude was a type of moral exhortation already present in the Old Testament. We find it especially in the Book of Psalms and the Wisdom literature. The first psalm begins, *"Happy are those who do not follow the advice of the wicked, or take the path that sinners tread, or sit in the seat of scoffers; but their delight is in the law of the Lord, and on his law they meditate day and night."*

Old Testament beatitudes can be divided into two types: instructions and promises. In the former, the instructions on good conduct, a moral tone is predominant. A blessing is pronounced upon a person who follows a virtuous line of action. These are the kind of beatitudes we find in Matthew.

The beatitudes of Luke, on the other hand, are promises looking forward to a future reversal for those who are now caught up in a situation of poverty and misery. Luke may be giving a more literal version of the original beatitudes as spoken by Jesus. The Lucan beatitudes, assuring the poor of God's help, would certainly have fitted easily on the lips of Jesus. He addressed his audience directly and guaranteed those who were suffering patiently that a better future awaited them.

While Luke explicitly refers to those who are materially poor and hungry, Matthew speaks of the poor "in spirit" and those who hunger and thirst "for righteousness." Instead of poverty in the physical sense, Matthew's beatitudes look for a virtuous disposition—inner detachment from earthly goods. Instead of looking for food, the disciples are exhorted to live in a state of energetic striving for holiness. This is the only hunger that is worthy of the followers of Jesus.

Matthew therefore describes the moral attitudes that are necessary to obtain entrance into the kingdom of heaven. His presentation puts the beatitudes of the Sermon on the Mount, as we could expect, squarely within the ethical teaching of the Old Testament.

Matthew has probably changed the style of the original beatitudes and made them applicable to the spiritual needs and moral endeavor of the members of his church. Rather than addressing the audience directly, the beatitudes in Matthew follow the form found in the psalms:

> Blessed are the poor in spirit, for theirs is the kingdom of heaven.
> Blessed are those who mourn, for they will be comforted.
> Blessed are the meek, for they will inherit the earth.
> Blessed are those who hunger and thirst for righteousness, for they will be filled.
> Blessed are the merciful, for they will receive mercy.
> Blessed are the pure in heart, for the will see God.
> Blessed are the peacemakers, for they will be called children of God. . . . (5:3–9)

Even in Matthew, however, the promise of future reversal remains intact. Those whom the world now considers miserable are blessed because they will be the ones who taste the joy of God's presence. Furthermore, the perseverance of the blessed will not be achieved by their own striving alone but will be the work of God's grace. Matthew brings this out by his use of what is called "the divine passive": *they will be comforted, they will be filled, they will receive mercy.* God is the understood agent of the coming reversal. So in Matthew too the fulfillment of the beatitudes is future, heavenly salvation.

Matthew's beatitudes set up entry into the kingdom of heaven as the supreme goal of life. Their structure makes this clear. The couplets forming each pronouncement first state an aspect of life that is blessed and then give a corresponding reward. The rewards mentioned are all substantially the same:

> It is not that the poor in spirit and the persecuted are assured of the Kingdom, while the mourners, the pure in heart, the peacemakers and so forth receive a variety of different blessings. Those who are blessed are not various types; they are the same people, described in a variety of ways, and the rewards of life in the Kingdom are shared by all—to be admitted to the kingdom of heaven means to be comforted, to have the deepest longings amply satisfied, to be acknowledged as sons of God, and to see him.[6]

Jesus and the Mosaic Law

After pronouncing the beatitudes Jesus exhorts his disciples to be the salt of the earth (5:13) and the light of the world (5:14). He calls them to witness by their good deeds to the reality of their commitment. Like Jesus, who is a light shining among the people living in darkness (4:16), the disciples must give moral direction to others by their example.

The public nature of their witness is shown by yet another reference to a mountain: The disciples are like a city perched on a hill, in full view of all who pass by. These comparisons lead to the declaration of Jesus on his relationship to the Mosaic law: *"Do not think that I have come to abolish the law or the prophets; I have come not to abolish but to fulfill. . . . For I tell you, unless your righteousness exceeds that of scribes and Pharisees, you will never enter the kingdom of heaven"* (Mt 5:17, 20).

Jesus, not the law, is the center of Matthew's Gospel. The teaching of Jesus, especially the Sermon on the Mount, is the ultimate norm of morality for the Christian disciple. The risen Christ makes this clear in the final mountain scene. So how is the law that was given to Moses to be seen in the light of the authority of Jesus?

In the Sermon Jesus asks from his disciples a righteousness greater than that of the Pharisees. The life of a Christian must overflow with the fullness of justice befitting the Lord he follows. The holiness of the disciples, their fidelity to the will of God, must go beyond the merely legalistic approach of the scribes.

This theme is developed as the Gospel proceeds and reaches a climax in the description of the final judgment. When the Son of man comes in his glory he will separate the sheep from the goats on the basis of how they have treated one another (25:31–46). The disciples have to practice the love shown by Jesus if they wish to be with him in the kingdom of heaven. Without such fidelity they will be sent to the eternal fire prepared for the devils and his angels.

We find, then, an interesting development in Matthew's teaching on the last judgment. The first Christian generation as represented by Paul stressed the imminent arrival of the final reckoning. In Matthew the strictness of the judgment, rather than its imminence, has become the spur to fidelity. This severity is especially directed to those who profess themselves disciples.

Jesus claimed that he had come to fulfill the law. He was convinced that he alone understood the true intention of the law. "Matthew wanted to demonstrate that the teaching of Jesus should not be understood as abrogating the law or correcting it. Rather, through his authority as messiah, Jesus teaches the ultimate intent and meaning of the law and thereby stands in radical continuity with the revelation of God's will in the law and the prophets."[7]

The authority of Jesus is illustrated in the six moral issues explicitly dealt with in the Sermon on the Mount—murder, adultery, divorce, oaths and vows, retaliation, and hatred of enemies (5:21–48). These teachings are sometimes referred to as "the six antitheses" because of the difference between what the Mosaic law held and what Jesus now says. They are concrete examples of the higher righteousness that Jesus has expounded in the beatitudes.

The first antithesis declares that not only murderers but even those who are angry with their brothers and sisters are liable to judgment. We should not approach God in our liturgies, says Jesus, until we are first reconciled to those at variance with us. This is clearly not a revocation of the law prohibiting murder and gives the original obligation an even deeper content.

Similarly, the second antithesis on the need for purity in thought as well as deed does not abolish but goes further than the Old Testament prohibition of adultery. Jesus calls for cleanliness of heart as well as the avoidance of illicit actions. The rabbis also denounced adultery of the heart and of the eye.

The third antithesis, on divorce, does in fact revoke the letter of the Mosaic dispensation that allowed divorce. Matthew agrees with Mark (10:2–12) and Paul (1 Cor 7:10–11) on this issue though he adds the qualifying clause that has become highly controversial, ". . . except on the ground of unchastity (*porneia*)."[8]

The fourth antithesis forbids the taking of oaths and the making of vows. Here we have another revocation of an Old Testament institution, the swearing of oaths. Such oaths were seen positively and sometimes directly commanded, as in the case of loss or injury to property (Ex 22:10–11).

The law of retaliation is revoked in the fifth antithesis. This is the clearest case of annulment in the six antitheses because the law of retaliation was mandatory. The reason for firmness in the matter of appropriate retaliation was to avoid unrestricted revenge and feuds. In this way Jesus is bringing the moderating tendencies of the law to their fullest conclusion.

Even though hatred of enemies was not directly commanded in the law, there was a popular belief that one need not love one's enemy. National enemies, in particular, were seen as the legitimate object of hate because they were also considered to be enemies of God. There are graphic descriptions in the psalms, for example 109:6–14, rejoicing in the destruction of enemies and their children. Indeed, the final antithesis, enjoining love of enemies, would probably have been the most startling of the six to those hearing them for the first time.

The six antitheses therefore demonstrate the attitude of Jesus to the Mosaic law. He does not simply reaffirm the law. He takes it through a process of refinement, which he says follows the true intentions of the divine lawmaker. This can mean revocation of the letter in some cases and a deeper penetration of the obligation in others. On his own authority Jesus brings the law to perfection.

We can see then that in Matthew the relationship of Jesus to the law is both positive and, above all, authoritative. As the Son of God, Jesus does not simply confirm and explain the law. "He fulfills it—with that prophetic fullness which sometimes goes beyond and antiquates the letter of the Law, just as it sometimes goes beyond and antiquates the original meaning of a prophecy."[9]

The most important of Jesus' five discourses in Matthew's Gospel, the Sermon on the Mount, ends with a reference to the amazement of the crowds. They are amazed not only at what Jesus has said but because he has taught with such force (7:28–29). Unlike the scribes, or even the Old Testament prophets, Jesus does not claim power from some external source. He preaches on his own authority.

Reflections

The law issue is fundamental to what Matthew has to say about discipleship. The followers of Christ take up a yoke that binds them to the risen Lord and the fulfillment of everything he has taught.

Jesus' moral authority is closely linked to Matthew's understanding of Jesus as Emmanuel, God with us. Jesus has the right to change the traditional interpretations of the Mosaic law. The presentation of Jesus as Emmanuel and his divine authority are linked to a third important dimension of Matthew's Gospel: the role of the church.

The Son of God has authority not only in himself, he also communicates a share of this authority to his disciples. They are given not only the mandate to teach all nations, there is also a promise that what they teach will be given his endorsement. Christ himself will underwrite their decisions.

These issues interlock at one critical point in Matthew—the confession of Simon Peter (16: 13–20). Adapting Mark to his own purposes, Matthew has Jesus ask the disciples who *they* think he is. Peter responds not only with a confession that Jesus is the Messiah but adds *"the Son of the living God."*

In response to Peter's declaration Jesus makes a statement on the structure of the community he is founding:

> And I tell you, you are Peter, and on this rock I will build my church, and the gates of Hades will not prevail against it. I will give you the keys of the kingdom of heaven, and whatever you bind on earth will be bound in heaven, and whatever you loose on earth will be loosed in heaven.

First of all, Peter is congratulated as being chosen to receive the revelation of the Father. He is given a title of his own. Like Abraham receiving a new name from God, Simon the son of Jonah will be called "the Rock." On this Rock Jesus will build his church, just as Abraham was the rock from which the people of Israel was cut (Isaiah 51:1–2).

The community of salvation founded by Jesus will have a firm earthly foundation in Peter. The position of Peter is reinforced by the use of another figure of speech—keys. Like the rock, the image of the keys is also taken from the Old Testament. Isaiah 22:15–25 describes the key of the house of David, symbol of authority, being given to a new steward. Thus the power Peter receives to open and shut, to bind and loose, is a share in Christ's own authority, given to him for the guidance of the other members of the church.

By carefully recasting the material at his disposal, Matthew has created a Gospel that gives us a profound statement on Christian discipleship. He had a very practical aim: To answer the pastoral needs of his community. He wanted to guide the disciples towards the perfection of holiness. The castigation of hypocrisy throughout the Gospel is a means of recalling contemporary Christians to their founding ideal. They too must reject double standards through a life of perfect conformity with the will of God.

The closing scene of the Gospel, the great commission, underpins this ideal by directing the faith of the disciples to the presence among them of the risen Christ. Acting through his chosen apostles, the Son of God will guide the future generations of the Christian community into the kingdom of the Father.

FOUR

Life in the Spirit

Discipleship and the Role of the Holy Spirit in Luke

"S ince many have undertaken to set down an orderly account of the events that have been fulfilled among us, just as they were handed on to us by those who from the beginning were eyewitnesses and servants of the word, I too decided, after investigating everything carefully from the very first, to write an orderly account for you, most excellent Theophilus, so that you may know the truth concerning the things about which you have been instructed" (Lk 1:1–4).

As we read Luke's first flowing sentence, we realize that we have come a long way from the language of Mark. The elegance of Luke is evident throughout the pages of his Gospel. The same polished grace is found in his second book, the Acts of the Apostles. For this reason Luke is considered the most accomplished writer in the New Testament.

The first four verses of the Gospel form the prologue to his two-volume work. Luke is the only New Testament author to begin his writing in such a formal manner.[1] The prologue of the Gospel is paralleled by the prologue of Acts (1:1–2). With these two similar introductions Luke indicates the continuity that he establishes between his first account, the story of Jesus, and his second, which narrates the history of the early church.

Writing most likely in the 80s of the first century, Luke was a third-generation Christian. He had to depend on the original eyewitnesses ("the servants of the word") who had passed down their traditions to posterity. As a good historian, he claims to have checked his sources before putting together the life of Jesus and the story of the early Christian community. Indeed, he believes that he has been able to produce a more complete account than his predecessors have.

He promises that his work will be thorough and systematic. He will go beyond what his predecessors have tried to do. There may even be a hint of superiority in the prologue: Luke believes he can produce a more satisfactory account for his contemporaries than what has been at their disposal up to that time.

However, if Luke intends to compose a history, he is not writing as a historian in the modern sense of the term. He is not primarily interested in giving a detached assessment of the facts. His clearly stated purpose is to provide a solid grounding for the Christian faith. He seeks to give firm assurance to his disciple, Theophilus, and his other readers for the beliefs in which they have been instructed.

Sacred history is Luke's theme, the history of God's dealings with his people. He is writing his account in the manner of the biblical authors. Unlike modern historians who concentrate their investigations upon the facts, the writers of the Bible were more interested in the meaning of the facts: What spiritual and moral lessons can be learned from them? Events are narrated for a purpose. The facts are the means by which God conveys his message. This does not mean that the facts are not important in themselves but the reader is cautioned not to take everything at face value. The author's intention and goals have to be kept continually in mind.

Luke's two volumes underline the continuity of Jesus' ministry, both with the activity of God in the old covenant and with what followed in the experiences of the early church. He adapted the earlier Gospel of Mark to his own interests. Like Matthew, he extended the timeline found in

Mark in two directions. First, he pushed his narrative of the life of Jesus back into the infancy. The first two chapters of Luke's Gospel, his most popular contribution to the life and spirituality of the church, link up Jesus and his family with the Old Testament. Second, after the resurrection, Jesus' activity is expanded to include a number of appearances. Luke's account of the ascension, featured in both his Gospel and Acts, ties the final appearance of Jesus directly into the history of the early church.

Luke wrote his Gospel around the same time as Matthew, and both authors prefaced the main gospel story with an infancy narrative. Yet, while the two compositions have many similarities, they also differ considerably. Matthew addresses a community still concerned with the Jewish law. Luke is preoccupied with the new churches springing up everywhere. He recounts the rapid spread of Christianity from tiny origins into all parts of the greater Gentile world. After the descent of the Holy Spirit upon the apostles, Luke enthusiastically describes how Jerusalem becomes the springboard for the spread of the gospel all the way to Rome. Luke is the historian of this Gentile mission.

But Luke is not only concerned with the past. He is also aware that the growth of the church calls for a fresh presentation of the gospel. A new adaptation of the message is needed for the very different situation in which Christians find themselves.

The synagogue is not the challenge. The Jews are no longer the people who need to be convinced. For this reason the Jewish origin of the gospel, especially what is found in the first two chapters of the infancy narrative, is dealt with in a manner quite different to that of Matthew. There is not the same insistence on the law; nor does Luke feel the need to justify everything he writes about Jesus the Christ with references to the fulfillment of Old Testament prophecies.

Unlike the first generation of Christians, many of Luke's converts are very much at home in the Roman world; the contemporary culture does not pose a threat to them. Luke's task is to show these disciples how their faith can be integrated into a more complete understanding of the milieu in which they live.

His immediate concern is to explain the global expansion of Christianity. For this reason he interprets the intentions of Jesus as geared from the start to a worldwide mission. In the passage that outlines the program of Jesus (4:16–30), Luke presents him in the fullness of his prophetical awareness proclaiming the universal nature of his task.

Although Luke's Gospel remains true to history by limiting the actual work of Jesus to his own country, Acts extends the scope of the mission until it reaches out to the whole world. At the same time, the historical difficulties that this extension of the mission to the pagans provoked among the members of the church are not ignored. They are incorporated into Luke's description of the first contacts of the disciples with the Gentile world and the debates that ensued before the issues arising from these encounters were finally resolved.

Luke's two volumes are able to connect the historical limits of Jesus' career with the full-blown Gentile mission of the church. They justify and uphold the coherence of what happened. Without the subsequent progress of the Christian community, the history of Jesus would have ended on Calvary. The church is the agent of God in the process of offering the salvation won by Jesus to men and women down through the ages.

The unity of Luke's double volume is achieved in two ways. There is, first of all, an external unity. More than any of the other evangelists, Luke is concerned with geography. For example, he extends Mark's story of Jesus on "the way" in the central section of his Gospel. The journey to Jerusalem occupies a central portion of the narrative.

The most obvious indication of Luke's geographical perspective is the manner in which the city of Jerusalem unites his Gospel and the Acts of the Apostles. The holy city is the place of destiny for Jesus and his community; Luke begins and ends his Gospel story in Jerusalem. The opening scene is Zechariah offering incense in the Temple. The child Jesus is taken to Jerusalem on at least two occasions and his encounter with the doctors foreshadows his future teaching in the Temple. Before the start of the public ministry the third temptation of Jesus takes place on the pinnacle of the Temple. The concluding ministry of Jesus in Jerusalem is the prelude to his death on Calvary. In Luke the resurrection appearances take place within the vicinity of Jerusalem. After the ascension the final scene of the Gospel tells how the Eleven returned to Jerusalem with great joy: *"And they were continually in the temple, blessing God"* (24:53).

Jerusalem, then, forms the geographical link between the Gospel and Acts. The account of the ascension from Jerusalem is repeated at the beginning of Acts. The disciples are told to await the coming of the Holy Spirit in Jerusalem. The city is the focal point from which the universal mission of the church radiates—even Paul has to return there. Jerusalem remains the mother-church as the Word of the Lord spreads to the ends of the earth. The city provides the external geographical link that binds Luke's story together.

But a second and even more important link in the history of Jesus and the first disciples is the inner power that binds them all together. From the beginning to the end of Luke's account the Holy Spirit is the divine presence that inspires both Jesus and the mission of the church. The Spirit is the divine force that guarantees continuity. Luke unites together the life of Jesus and the early history of the Christian community through the presence of the Spirit. Jesus' mission is inaugurated by the descent of the Spirit at his baptism. The mission of the church begins with the Spirit's descent at Pentecost and will endure until the end of the world. The unity between the mission of Jesus and that of the church is indicated by the two descents of the Spirit.

In the life of Jesus, the Spirit's descent serves to interpret his baptism (3: 21–22). At the founding moment of the church, the descent of the Spirit is interpreted as a baptism of the disciples (Acts 1:5). The activity of Jesus and the work of the church are closely bound together; the Spirit guides both the ministry and preaching of Jesus. Afterwards, when instead of being the one who proclaims, Jesus is the one proclaimed, the Spirit guides the apostolic labors of the disciples as well.

The Spirit Gives Life
to Jesus and His Followers

None of the other evangelists gives such a leading role to the Holy Spirit as does Luke. He upholds the prominent position of the Spirit both in the Gospel and Acts. The Spirit is mentioned seventeen times in Luke's Gospel and fifty-seven times in Acts. Even more significant than the high number of references is their position in the story. The Spirit is especially active at important moments—the description of the birth of Jesus in chapters 1 and 2, the temptation scene, the start of the public ministry, the ascension and, of course, Pentecost. All the important stages of the history that are played out in Luke are set in motion by the presence of the Holy Spirit.

One point needs to be stated lest we read too much into Luke's references to the Holy Spirit. These descriptions, as indeed the other references we find to the Spirit in the New Testament, should not be read with the eyes of later generations. Luke does not give us a doctrine of the Holy Spirit such as we find in the ensuing Councils of the church in later centuries. He does not refer to the Spirit as the third person of the Trinity, for example. This later doctrine was built on the biblical foundations given by Luke and Paul and can be said to develop them to their full implications. Trinitarian theology comes from generations of reflection and controversy.

Luke usually describes the action of the Holy Spirit with the language of the Old Testament. There the Spirit is the irresistible force of God's action in the world—the Spirit is active in human beings as a prophetic voice and in nature as a creative power. Luke speaks about the Spirit more as a divine life-giving energy than a divine being. However, personal actions are occasionally attributed to the Spirit, as in Luke 2:26, which speaks of Simeon being told about the Messiah by the Holy Spirit.

Luke refers twice to the Spirit as "the Father's promise" (Lk 24:49; Acts 1:4). He may have had in mind the promises found in Ezekiel, who spoke about a new outpouring of the divine Spirit in the latter days: *"He must never drink wine or strong drink; even before his birth he will be filled with the Holy Spirit"* (Lk 1:15).

When the arrival of John the Baptist is announced, his father is told that John will be filled with the Holy Spirit from birth. As the one who is to introduce the key figure of the gospel and foreshadow Jesus' public ministry, John shares in the manifestation of the Spirit that is to guide both Jesus and the community of the church. Because John is consecrated to God, the Spirit of the Lord possesses him from his mother's womb.

Much more important, of course, is the role of the Spirit in the conception of the child Jesus. The Spirit is most active in Mary, coming upon her to bring about the virginal conception. The angel said to her: *"The Holy Spirit will come upon you, and the power of the Most High will overshadow you"* (1:35). Following the usage of the Old Testament, the "Holy Spirit" and "the power of the Most High" are parallel expressions. The Spirit is understood as God's creative ability. The Spirit will come to overshadow Mary in a special way. Therefore the child she bears will be holy, that is to say, consecrated to the service of the Lord.

The newborn Jesus is brought to the Temple to fulfill the requirements of the law. The devout and aged Simeon meets him. Like the prophets before him, the old man is endowed with the Spirit of God who had made known to him that he would not die until he had seen the Messiah. By the same Spirit, he is guided to Jesus and makes his utterance regarding the child (2:25–27). In Luke's view there was nothing accidental about this encounter.

Luke's story moves quickly on to the ministry of Jesus. As part of the preparation for his mission Jesus probably became, at least for a while, a disciple of John the Baptist. His baptism in the Jordan was a form of public association with John. At that moment *"the Holy Spirit descended upon him in bodily form like a dove"* (3:22). Luke has made a number of changes in Mark's presentation of the baptism of Jesus but has kept intact the detail about the descent of the Spirit in the form of a dove.

The main purpose of the baptismal scene in Luke's Gospel is not to proclaim Jesus as the Son of God or tell us that he possesses the Spirit. We already know this from the infancy narrative. What the Spirit does at this point in Luke's narrative is to consecrate Jesus for his task. The descent of the Holy Spirit is the immediate preparation for Jesus' public ministry. The later Lucan reflection on the baptismal scene (in Acts 10:37–38) will note how God anointed Jesus *"with the Holy Spirit and with power."* The timing of the descent of the Holy Spirit is suggested in the following verse indicating that Jesus was about thirty years old when he began his preaching and healing. This was a very important moment in his life.

The dove has become a traditional symbol for the Holy Spirit. Yet, even though all three synoptists (Matthew, Mark, and Luke) have portrayed the dove as a sign of the Spirit's presence, there is no clarity with regard to the origins of the symbol. One possible explanation is the dove released by Noah after the flood. It was the sign of a new beginning for the human race (Gen 8:11). This would fit in well with what is about to happen in the ministry of Jesus.

Luke is conveying the reality of the Spirit's presence by stressing that the dove came down upon Jesus in bodily form. "It fits in with the greater attention shown to the Spirit in the Lucan writings than in either of the other Synoptic evangelists. In light of the prominence that the Spirit has in Lucan theology, this detail is not surprising."[2]

The Spirit comes upon Jesus in the form of a dove as his preaching begins. Later on, in the second great outpouring at Pentecost, the Holy Spirit will come upon the disciples in the form of a mighty wind and tongues as of fire to strengthen them for their worldwide mission (Acts 2:2–4).

Closely linked to Jesus' baptism is the final act of preparation for his public ministry. Filled with the Holy Spirit he is led into confrontation with the forces of evil. Because he is endowed with divine power he is able to overcome the devil in three seductive encounters. These temptations sum up the hostility, opposition, and rejection that Jesus and his disciples will have to face throughout their lives. Despite the enticement to use his power in an extraordinary fashion, Jesus remains faithful to the Father's will and resists the allurements of the devil.

Jesus' first discourse in the synagogue at Nazareth outlines the objectives of his ministry (4:16–30). We shall look at this scene in the next section. For the moment we note that the Spirit is of particular importance as the work of Jesus begins. Quoting Isaiah 61:1, Jesus proclaims that the Spirit of the Lord is upon him and has anointed him.

At the end of Luke's Gospel Jesus tells the Eleven to await "the Father's promise." At the beginning of Acts this instruction is repeated, *"for John baptized with water, but you will be baptized with the Holy Spirit"* (1:5).

What the Spirit did for Jesus at his baptism in the form of a dove is repeated for his followers at Pentecost. The church too is consecrated for mission through the descent of the Holy Spirit, this time in the form of fiery tongues. The second coming is not an individual experience, as in the case of Jesus—the whole community is consecrated. A new age is inaugurated when the fire of the Spirit is poured out upon the disciples in the upper room.

The descent of the Holy Spirit described in the second chapter of Acts is the starting point for everything that happens afterwards. Through this empowerment the disciples are commissioned to be apostles. The Holy Spirit will be the guiding force behind their labors. It will direct their activities and even prevent certain ventures from being undertaken, as in 16:7.

Furthermore, the Spirit is seen at Pentecost and in the rest of Acts not only as the creative presence of God but also as "the Spirit of Jesus" (16:7). Through his Spirit, Jesus will continue to be present among his followers, even though he is physically absent from them.

After the descent of the Spirit at Pentecost, the next significant event in Acts is the conversion of Paul. He is the hero of the second part of the book and he too is liberally endowed with the gifts of the Holy Spirit. Despite initial hesitations, Ananias baptizes Saul but first invokes the Holy Spirit upon him: *"He laid his hands on Saul and said, 'Brother Saul, the Lord Jesus, who appeared to you on your way here, has sent me so that you may regain your sight and be filled with the Holy Spirit.' And immediately something like scales fell from his eyes, and his sight was restored"* (9:17–18). Through this anointing Paul becomes the "chosen instrument" to carry the name of Jesus to Gentiles, kings, and the people of Israel.

In the age inaugurated by the Holy Spirit, the promises of old are not only fulfilled in individual cases, important though these may be; the whole people of God are invested with a new dynamism. The most significant outcome of this power is the startling growth of the Christian church. Luke likes to tell us how many thousands were converted by the words of the apostles. Even Paul's conversion, narrated three times in Acts, is portrayed as a moment of importance for the whole community. Through him the Spirit will guide the young church as it takes its first steps in the direction of a world mission.

The Holy Spirit's function is not limited to purely external manifestations. Luke also shows how the spiritual lives of the disciples are transformed by the inner action of God's Spirit. In addition to describing the preaching of the Word to the pagan world, Acts stresses the personal bonds that existed in the early days among the members of the church. Luke describes the lifestyle of the disciples in Acts as one of sharing at both the spiritual and material levels. He sums up the Jerusalem church in a portrait which, with a certain nostalgia, he obviously considered the ideal for his own day: *"They devoted themselves to the apostles' teaching and fellowship, to the breaking of bread and the prayers"* (2:42). These four elements cover the essentials of the Christian life. The stories of Barnabas and the couple Ananias and Sapphira illustrate both fidelity and betrayal of these ideals. The latter, through their hypocrisy and avarice, draw down the divine wrath upon their heads (5:1–11).

The prayer life of the community is mentioned at various points in Acts. It is first introduced to describe the attitude of the apostles as they await the coming of the Holy Spirit: *"All these were constantly devoting themselves to prayer, together with certain women, including Mary the mother of Jesus"* (1:14).

The need to maintain their prayer life is the important factor in the decision of the apostles to institute the deacons; *"while we, for our part, will devote ourselves to prayer and to serving the word"* (6:4). By highlighting the devotion of the apostles, Luke parallels in Acts what he has already said in the Gospel about the role of prayer in the life of Jesus.

"The Spirit of the Lord Is upon Me"

Filled with the power of the Holy Spirit, Jesus comes to the synagogue of Nazareth. There he outlines the program of work and preaching that will unfold throughout the Gospel:

> When he came to Nazareth, where he had been brought up, he went to the synagogue on the sabbath day, as was his custom. He stood up to read, and the scroll of the prophet Isaiah was given to him. He unrolled the scroll and found the place where it was written: "The Spirit of the Lord is upon me, because he has anointed me to bring good news to the poor. He has sent me to proclaim release to the captives and recovery of sight to the blind, to let the oppressed go free, to proclaim the year of the Lord's favor." (Lk 4: 16–19)

Luke has elaborated Mark's simpler account of this opening scene of the public ministry. Mark had said that Jesus was teaching in the synagogue of Nazareth but did not mention the Spirit nor say anything about the content of the teaching (6:1–6). Luke takes Mark's account a step further: He underlines the role of the Spirit in the preaching of Jesus and mentions the year of the Lord's favor. The era of salvation has begun through the preaching of good news to the poor and the performance of mighty works.

The Spirit had already consecrated Jesus at his baptism. Now we hear how the Spirit is working within him and how this will effect his ministry. The words quoted by Jesus from the Old Testament are a combination of Isaiah 61:1–2 and 58:6.[3] The texts from Isaiah point to Jesus as a fulfillment of the promises. Anointed with the Spirit, Jesus appears as the long-awaited prophet. He brings the message of salvation to his people. The citizens of Nazareth are the first to hear the good news. But as the narrative proceeds, their initial enthusiasm turns to hostility. Their negative reaction to the young preacher is the first warning of the rejection that he will face among his own. In this overture to the public ministry Nazareth takes on a symbolic role for the whole Jewish nation.

At the beginning of the Gospel the holy man Simeon had described Jesus as a light of revelation to the Gentiles (2:32). Now in the synagogue of Nazareth Jesus declares that he has come to give a universal message. Needless to say, apart from a few isolated contacts with the pagan world, this intention remained unfulfilled in Jesus' lifetime. But in his second volume, the book of Acts, Luke will show how the apostles set about a global enterprise to bring the deepest intentions of Jesus to fulfillment.

Nazareth is a place where the message of Jesus is rejected. In Acts the city of Rome becomes the symbol of success and acceptance. The capital of the empire is the final destination of Paul's mission. His presence there is proof of the all-embracing nature of the church's mission. Neither geographical nor social barriers bind the good news.

Preaching, healing, and exorcism are the powers that the Spirit imparts to Jesus and his disciples. In Luke's vision the work of Jesus and the work of the church are in perfect continuity. They are both concerned with the welfare of the people of God in all its dimensions. Healing of mind and body goes hand in hand with the preaching of the gospel. The needy, the dispossessed, and the poor are therefore the primary recipients of the salvation announced by Jesus.

"Good news to the poor"

Luke paints an idyllic picture of the Christian community in Jerusalem as we noted earlier. For him the sharing of material goods had an important place in the life of the disciples. It was the outward expression of their interior bond of unity. No writer of the New Testament speaks about the use of material goods and wealth to the same extent as Luke. "Obviously, he is not satisfied with what he has seen of the Christian use of wealth in his ecclesial community and makes use of sayings of Jesus to correct attitudes within it."[4]

In Mark there are warnings on the danger of wealth; Jesus speaks about the greater ease of a camel passing through a needle than a rich man entering the kingdom of God. So the emphasis on detachment from possessions is not Luke's exclusive preserve. He put a particular stress on this aspect of discipleship probably because he believed the Christians of his own day needed the reminder.

Luke's "option for the poor," as it is called, runs right through both his Gospel and his history of the apostolic church. It can be seen in the infancy narrative when, instead of the wise men, as in Matthew, poor shepherds are the first to come to adore the Christ child. In her hymn of praise the mother of Jesus thanks God for filling the poor with good things while the rich are sent away empty-handed.

We can detect a twofold attitude in Luke to material possessions: A moderate attitude, which advocates a prudent use of material goods and the giving of assistance to the needy; and a more radical approach that advocates the renunciation of possessions.[5]

The *moderate* attitude, recommending a prudent use of material wealth, can be seen in the Gospel when John the Baptist tells those coming to him for advice to share their clothes with those who have none (3:11). The most unusual example of this approach is the parable of the dishonest manager and the application Jesus makes of it: *"And I tell you, make friends for yourselves by means of dishonest wealth so that when it is gone, they may welcome you into the eternal homes"* (16:9).

Jesus himself and his disciples benefited from the generosity of the women of Galilee *"who provided for them out of their resources"* (8:3). This tradition is continued in Acts where the apostles are continually supported in their mission by wealthy people. Dorcas, who went about providing relief for the poor, was rewarded by being raised up to life by Peter (9:36–42).

The *radical* attitude to the goods of the world is reflected in such texts as the missionary advice to take nothing for the journey (9:3). We see it, above all, in the exhortation to prospective disciples: *"Sell your possessions, and give alms. Make purses for yourselves that do not wear out, an unfailing treasure in heaven, where no thief comes near and no moth destroys"* (12:33). In the same vein Jesus tells the crowd quite categorically, *"none of you can become my disciple if you do not give up all your possessions"* (14:33).

The more radical attitude is prevalent in Acts. The ideal of the early Christian community was to share land and houses together. Because of this, says Luke, there were no needy members among the disciples. The glowing picture painted in the first chapters of Acts is darkened by the deception of Ananias and his wife Sapphira and we may be nearer to the situation that actually prevailed in the account of the dispute between the Hebrew and Greek Christians over the distribution of aid to their widows (6:1–7).

By describing his mission in terms of good news for the poor, Jesus directs our attention to the plight of the poor.

The promise of good news for the poor is an initial summary of what will be developed later in Luke's Gospel. In the report Jesus sends back to John the Baptist, he informs him that *"the blind receive their sight, the lame walk, the lepers are cleansed, the deaf hear, the dead are raised, the poor have good news brought to them"* (7:22).

Who exactly are the poor to whom the good news is preached? A recent study of Luke notes that a curious feature of his Gospel is that having been anointed to proclaim good news to the poor, Jesus is found repeatedly frequenting the homes of the wealthy![6] In the chapter following the proclamation at Nazareth, we read that Levi held a great banquet for Jesus at his house (5:29). If the poor are taken purely in economic terms by Luke then the lack of coherence between the mission statement of Jesus and the ensuing ministry is puzzling.

One solution is that the social situation for which Luke was writing differed from that of Jesus. The community had evolved considerably in the ensuing half century. The evangelist's intention was to make the tradition of Jesus' association with the poor challenge the more sophisticated community of his own day. In this way he hoped that the destitute would continue to be the object of concern and active compassion.

Another commentator concludes that Luke was concerned above all with people being excluded, because of their lack of social standing, from the circles of power and prestige. In contrast to this, Jesus proclaims a new era that embraces the poor and those defined as outsiders.[7] The overturning of the old order is also proclaimed in Mary's hymn of praise. She contrasts the fate of the powerful with the elevation of the humble and the lowly (1:53).

The story of Zacchaeus shows that material possessions were not the only criterion of social status in the world of Jesus. Although he was wealthy, Zacchaeus was considered an outsider because of his exaction as a tax collector. When the crowd begins to mutter because Jesus had gone to the house of a sinner, he tells them that salvation had come to Zacchaeus's house because he too *"is a son of Abraham"* (19:9).

So in the third Gospel "poor" becomes a definition for those of lowly status—those excluded from positions of respect and authority. Although the term is not without economic significance, the wider meaning of exclusion is paramount. "Good news to the poor" is first of all the hopeful message of Jesus to the dispossessed.

In the mission statement of Jesus, the poor are the financially deprived but also prisoners, the blind, and the oppressed. The references to Elijah and Elisha (4:24–28) are significant. With the example of their ministry to outsiders, Jesus is saying, in effect, that "good news to the poor" embraces the widow, the unclean, and the Gentiles.

Indeed, it was the implication that they had lost their privileged status in the eyes of God that caused the good citizens of Nazareth to become furious and drive Jesus out of town (4:29).

"The year of the Lord's favor"

Filled with the power of the Holy Spirit, Jesus announces the year acceptable to the Lord. The year of the Lord's favor is the time God has appointed to bring about his saving action. Concretely, the allusion is to the "year of jubilee," the year of liberation appointed by God in the Old Testament: *"And you shall hallow the fiftieth year and you shall proclaim liberty throughout the land to all its inhabitants. It shall be a jubilee for you: you shall return, every one of you, to your property and every one of you to your family"* (Lev 25:10).

The Jubilee year was the seventh sabbatical year held every fifty years. During this time the fields lay fallow, exiles returned to their homes, debts were remitted, and slaves set free. The year of Jubilee was a period dedicated to the remembrance of the Lord's sovereignty over the land, the people and their possessions.

There are no indications from the Old Testament that the directives of the Jubilee year regarding the cancellation of debts and the liberation of slaves were actually carried out. The way society evolved would have made such prescriptions impracticable. So "the year of the Lord's favor" was eventually understood to mean a future time of divine favor and blessing.

In his mission statement Jesus refers to the hope of the afflicted and brokenhearted to characterize the period set in motion by his preaching. Having been consecrated with the Spirit, he initiates the era of salvation promised by Isaiah and the other prophets.

Onto the early, limited understanding of the Jubilee year a more universal hope is grafted. The year of divine favor will not only affect the people of Israel but will bring blessings to all nations. In this adaptation of Isaiah's dream there is no mention of "the day of vengeance" foretold by the prophet (61:2). A reference to vengeance would not have been an appropriate way to describe the saving work of Jesus.

"Today this scripture has been fulfilled in your hearing" (4:21)

This is an emphatic statement. It not only refers to the actual day Jesus spoke but also and especially to the dawning of the time of sight, release, and liberty predicted by Isaiah. The "year of the Lord's favor" has arrived in the person and work of Jesus. Divine blessings come upon the world through his ministry. They will continue in the life of the church and be fully realized at the second coming.

Like Paul before him, Luke had to deal with a problem that troubled the Christians of the first century—the delay of the final coming promised by Jesus. The "today" of 4:21 is thus an example of how Luke redirects the emphasis in many of Jesus' sayings. Along with bringing to mind a future reckoning, the call for true conversion of heart is shown to be a valid guide for daily conduct among the men and women of his own generation. "This subtle shift directs Christian attention from the following of Christ in view of an imminent reckoning to an understanding of

Jesus' conduct as an inspiration and guide for Christian life."[8]

Jesus' words in the synagogue of Nazareth have an important place in Luke's presentation of the good news. His mission is empowered by the Holy Spirit and involves not only preaching but also healing and an active option for the poor. From the beginning of his ministry Jesus points beyond the confines of Israel and reveals his intention to touch the whole world.

"The Power of the Most High Shall Overshadow You"

One of the groups that could have been classified as "poor" in the time of Jesus was women. They were among the oppressed and excluded of the day. Yet in Luke's Gospel women are portrayed in a very positive light. They play a bigger part in Luke/Acts than in any other book of the New Testament. Not only are women mentioned more frequently in Luke, they are given a special place in the origins of Christianity. This is particularly true of Mary, the mother of Jesus, but the other women of the story also appear in significant roles.

Women as Disciples in Luke/Acts

Luke reports that Jesus went from town to town and village to village proclaiming the good news of the kingdom: *"The twelve were with him, as well as some women who had been cured of evil spirits and infirmities; Mary, called Magdalene, from whom seven demons had gone out, and Joanna, the wife of Herod's steward, Chuza, and Susanna, and many others, who provided for them out of their resources"* (Lk 8:1–3). The fact that women were accepted as followers of Jesus alongside men was quite exceptional. "Such a closeness to women was unthinkable in the Judaism of that time, but Jesus accepts them into his following."[9]

The women from Galilee accompanied Jesus all the way to Jerusalem and stayed to watch on Calvary (Lk 23:49). After following Joseph of Arimathea and seeing the tomb where the body of Jesus was laid, they went home and prepared spices and perfumes for the final anointing of the body. They came to the tomb on the first day of the week and were the first to hear the news of the resurrection: *"And returning from the tomb, they told all this to the eleven and to all the rest"* (Lk 24:9). Because of their fidelity to Jesus during his earthly ministry and their witness to the death, burial, and resurrection, the Galilean women were a crucial link in transmitting the Easter message.

The Acts of the Apostles leaves us in no doubt that right from the beginning women were beside men in their apostolic labors. As the apostles awaited the coming of the Holy Spirit they joined in prayer, *"together with certain women, including Mary the mother of Jesus"* (1:14).

Women are woven into the fabric of the church as disciples from the very beginning. Luke delights in recounting that large numbers of men and women were led to faith in the Lord. Individual women are highlighted because of their contribution to the missionary cause. Lydia, Paul's first convert in Greece, offered him and his companions the hospitality of her home (Acts 16:14–15). Similarly, Priscilla and Aquila gave active support and accompanied Paul on his journey from Corinth to Ephesus (Acts 18:19–20). The house of Mark's mother was a place of gathering for prayer and other house churches may have formed around leading women disciples.

The quality of discipleship that these women reveal is also significant. They have a particular sensitivity to suffering and injustice. The women who accompany Jesus from Galilee to Jerusalem remain faithful to the end. On the way to Calvary women are the only ones to show compassion through their tears and laments.

In the story of Martha and Mary (10:38–42) Luke gives the reader an insight into discipleship and a teaching about prayer through the different attitudes of two women. A

basic requirement of the Christian vocation is the willingness to listen to the Word of God, as Mary shows during
Jesus' visit. Her attentive listening is more important than
the busy activity of her sister. Mary is an example of the
true disciple. Like the mother of Jesus, she has the ability to
ponder and penetrate the Word of God more deeply than
those around her. For this reason Jesus says she has chosen
the better part.

Another woman held up as an example for the followers of Jesus is the widow in the parable of the godless judge
(18:1–5). Her insistent prayer shows how the oppressed
should cry out to God. The determination of her prayer
echoes the strong women of the Bible who cried out to God
for deliverance.

Mary, the Perfect Disciple

In the Gospel of Luke Jesus' mother is presented as the
ideal disciple. This was the conclusion of an ecumenical
task force studying the role of Mary in the New Testament.[10] Although women are included among the disciples
and figure prominently in the narrative, the capacity to
respond faithfully is most fully realized in Mary. Luke sees
Mary as a model for all believers. She is the first Christian
disciple. She fulfills the essential requirement of true discipleship—attentiveness to the Word of God. This docility
enables the Spirit to work fruitfully through her.[11]

The portrayal of Mary in the infancy narrative is part of
a dramatic composition written by Luke rather than a
detailed eye-witness account that gives us precise information. In the dialogue between Mary and the angel Gabriel,
Mary's question *"How can this be?"* is a device commonly
used by biblical writers to open the door to a fuller explanation. Mary's words are not to be taken as an objection or
protest.[12]

Luke presents the relationship of Jesus with his mother
and family differently than Mark. Whereas Mark seems to
put a distance between them, Luke softens this picture con-

siderably. The hearers of the Word of God do not replace the mother of Jesus as his real family as Mark seems to suggest in 3:31–35. Luke leaves the reader certain that the mother and brothers of Jesus are among those who hear the Word of God and put it into practice (8:21). The mother and family of Jesus are prominent among those who pray together in preparation for the coming of the Holy Spirit (Acts 1:14).

Two other women sing Mary's praises in Luke's Gospel. The first is her cousin Elizabeth: *"Blessed are you among women, and blessed is the fruit of your womb. . . . And blessed is she who believed that there would be a fulfillment of what was spoken to her by the Lord"* (1:42, 45).

Inspired by the Holy Spirit, Elizabeth calls Mary "blessed" and again explains to the reader how she has become the mother of Jesus. The conception of Mary's child is not through any physical contribution on the part of a man, but the result of her faith in the promise of the Lord. Mary's fidelity has brought God's promise to fulfillment. She stands in sharp contrast to Elizabeth's husband who did not believe the message of the angel.

Elizabeth's canticle echoes the praises sung about Judith in the Old Testament. This valiant woman was God's instrument in delivering the people from a powerful enemy (Jdt 13:18). Mary too, because of her obedience to the angel's word, is the mighty instrument of divine mercy. God is again using the weak of the earth to confound the strong. Mary is blessed because the child she will bear is blessed. Her obedience to the plan of salvation, not her personal attractiveness, is the true source of her greatness.

The other woman who sings the praise of Mary in Luke's Gospel is among the crowd listening to the words of Jesus: *"Blessed is the womb that bore you and the breasts that nursed you!"* (11:27). Only Luke records this episode. It continues the praise given to Mary in the infancy narrative. The incident begins with a blessing on her motherhood, but Jesus' answer points in the direction of Mary's true greatness: *"Blessed rather are those who hear the word of God and obey it!"* (11:28).

Again Luke informs his community that Mary is worthy of praise not just because she gave physical birth to Jesus but because she has listened to the Word of God and believed. This is what makes her the first of the disciples and the perfect model of the faithful Christian.

Reflections

In response to the words of Elizabeth, Mary, herself filled with the Holy Spirit, proclaims the praises of God in her own canticle of thanksgiving, the Magnificat.

Mary's song of praise, like the other canticles in Luke, contains many echoes of the Old Testament. She is here a representative of those early Christian Jews who identified themselves with the "poor ones," the *Anawim* of postexilic times. They were distinguished not simply from the rich, but above all from the arrogant and self-sufficient who showed no need of God.[13]

Esteeming Mary as the first Christian disciple, Luke "has placed the hymn on her lips and thus given her the role as spokeswoman of the Anawim."[14] As the faithful servant of the Lord, Mary was obedient to his word, and believed in the fulfillment of the promise that would fill her womb with the presence of the Messiah and make her blessed among women.

Already at the moment of his conception, and not just through death and resurrection, Jesus is the Savior of the world (2:11). Having been overshadowed by the power of the Spirit, Mary can voice the joy of salvation, which the poor of God experience when they proclaim Jesus as the Messiah. Mary is "full of grace" and her song of thanksgiving gives the reasons why she has found favor with God.

Mary's song of thanksgiving is therefore both an overture and a summing up of Luke's Gospel. Her song directs our attention to the child she has conceived and also anticipates the preaching of Jesus on wealth and power. These are not real values at all because they have no standing in

God's sight. Because Mary is the first Christian disciple, it is fitting that Luke places on her lips the sentiments that will distinguish all true followers of her Son.

The Vine and the Branches

Jesus and His Disciples in the Fourth Gospel

The word disciple is found more frequently in John than in any of the other Gospels. Right from the beginning of his ministry, Jesus is accompanied by a band of followers. Their calling is described in a lengthy section of John's opening chapter. The first two are invited to "come and see" where Jesus lives and, after spending an afternoon in his company, they quickly bring two more. The next day Jesus invites Philip to follow him. These initial encounters are capped with the conversion of the true Israelite, Nathaniel (1:29–51).

Unlike Mark who depicts Jesus frequently upbraiding "the Twelve" for their lack of faith, John underlines the belief of the disciples. At the wedding feast of Cana where, for the first time, Jesus revealed his glory, John tells us that "his disciples believed in him" (2:11). At the end of the same chapter, during the cleansing of the Temple, the disciples are the only ones who interpret the event properly. When many turn away after the teaching on the bread of life, the core of disciples holds firm. Peter speaks for them all when he renews his commitment to Jesus: *"We have come to believe and know that you are the Holy One of God"* (6:69).

The portrayal of the disciples in John is not totally positive, however. Their faith too is inadequate at times. During the Last Supper Thomas and Philip are reproved for their lack of perception. Thomas's resistance to the resurrection message is used by the evangelist to introduce the final teaching of his Gospel: *"Blessed are those who have not seen and yet have come to believe"* (20:29).

Along with the chosen band of the Twelve, other people are drawn into Jesus' circle. At the beginning of chapter 4 the reader is informed that Jesus was making more disciples than John the Baptist. Chapter 6 refers to a large number of disciples; as a result of the instruction on the bread of life *"many of his disciples turned back and no longer went about with him"* (6:66).

The man healed of blindness in chapter 9 becomes a disciple of Jesus. He stands in sharp contrast to the Pharisees, who scornfully reject the testimony of his cure and refuse to accept Jesus by claiming to be disciples of Moses. After Jesus' death his body is taken away by Joseph of Arimathea, a disciple of Jesus, *"though a secret one, because of his fear of the Jews"* (19:38).

Discipleship is a subject running right through the fourth Gospel. "In a document which looks back at Jesus' activity on earth and introduces the theme of the present into this perspective, the first and most obvious datum that has to be taken into consideration is the concept of discipleship or the gospel's understanding of the group of disciples."[1]

Yet, though discipleship is a major consideration of the fourth Gospel, it is not the central theme. There is really only one theme in John, a theme that absorbs all others: The person of Jesus Christ. All the Gospels are naturally concerned with Jesus, but none of the first three attains the single-mindedness of John. While the synoptists (Matthew, Mark, and Luke) speak about the good news of the kingdom of God, the last Gospel concentrates on the divine personality of Christ. Jesus not only speaks about the kingdom; in him the kingdom is already present.

The perspective that John adopts in his portrait of Jesus is a total emphasis on his status as the Word, the only Son

of God. The opening verses or prologue of the Gospel set
the tone for this deep concentration (1:1–18). In comparison, the introduction to Luke's Gospel does not even mention the name of Jesus. Luke's concern is to give a reliable
account of *the events* that have taken place at the beginning
of the Christian era.

Unlike the speeches of Matthew that cover a variety of
topics, the discourses in John have an exclusive aim: To
build up faith in the person of Jesus Christ. One can speak
of a "christological implosion" in John, meaning by this
that all other themes are absorbed into the person of Jesus.
Like a black hole in space, the fourth Gospel's attention to
Jesus the divine Word of God absorbs the other teachings
into its gravitational pull.[2]

Even more insistently than the other evangelists, John
emphasizes that the essential requirement of a true follower is belief in the person of Jesus. The reinforcement of
faith as the purpose of the book is stated unambiguously in
the conclusion: *"Now Jesus did many other signs in the presence of his disciples, which are not written in this book. But these
are written so that you may come to believe that Jesus is the Messiah, the Son of God"* (20:30–31). John speaks not only to his
own generation; he addresses the same message to his
future readers.

The evangelist wants to make the earthly Jesus present
as the living and life-giving Christ. To this end the discourses are more a reflection on who Jesus is rather than an
instruction on the moral consequences of following him.
The miracles too are not just great deeds that herald the
kingdom of God; they are "signs" pointing to the nature of
the One who has come down from heaven.

Faith is the necessary response to Jesus. This faith is an
act of commitment. To bring out the dynamic aspect of
faith, John uses the verb "to believe in" rather than the
noun "faith." To believe is not only to trust in Jesus and
have confidence in him but also requires a full acceptance
of what he claims to be. Believing in Jesus is a dynamic
action as well as an intellectual assent.

Christian faith is life-giving. Through abiding in the Word we become children of God. Because of our new status, the gift that Christ brings to his disciples—and to us— is most aptly summed up in one word: Life.

In John's Gospel everything that Jesus says and does, all that he reveals and accomplishes, are ordained to the life of the world. Jesus has come to give his disciples life to the full (10:10). The "christological implosion," therefore, by concentrating on the divine power of the Word of God, assures us that by his very presence Christ is giving life to the world.

Who Jesus is and what he achieves are inseparably joined together in the thought of the fourth evangelist. From the divine person of Christ flow the profound sayings and powerful signs that call for a response of faith. Those who do not believe in him are cut off from the divine truth he brings. They cannot enter into the way of life. Instead they bring judgment and condemnation upon themselves.

"I am the way, and the truth and the life" (14:6). This cluster of images is the best-known example of a form of address that has a unique place in the fourth Gospel. The "I am" sayings of Jesus, found at significant points in the narrative, explore with a variety of expressions who he is and what he has come to do. The discourses of Jesus in the Gospel frequently hinge on such "I am" sayings. Jesus reinforces his claim to the faith of the disciples by referring to himself with different figures of speech.

The "I am" sayings provide us with a key to understanding the special relationship that exists between the Son of man and his followers. We shall therefore look at three of the most popular of these sayings to see what insight they give us on discipleship.

"I Am the Vine, You Are the Branches"

Paul and the synoptics speak of Jesus coming in his glory at the end of time to lead his followers into the kingdom of God. For them eternal life is strictly a gift to be received in the age to come. John, on the other hand, puts the emphasis firmly in the present. Eternal life has already begun for the disciples through their faith in Jesus Christ.

The allegory of the vine and the branches is an illustration of the new life Christ communicates to his followers. It is the dominant figure of speech at the center of the Last Supper discourse (15:1–8). During this final and most important instruction, Jesus compares his beloved disciples to the branches of a vine. They must stay close in order to draw strength from him, the source of life.

To understand the allegory aright, "we must realize that it does not draw attention to the vine with regard to its fruit, or to the wine that it bestows, but simply to the tree itself with its shoots, and that the shoots are perfuse with vital power from it; from the tree they receive their power to grow and to bear fruit, and they wither away if they are cut off from it: *'The vine is the tree of life.'"*[3]

We can trace the origins of the vine allegory back to the Old Testament. Israel was frequently compared to a fruitful or, even more frequently, to an unproductive vineyard. Psalm 80 calls on God to have pity on the vine his own right hand has planted but which has been cut down by the impious. The prophet Jeremiah was commanded by God to search carefully for the faithful few among the vine-rows and strip away the branches that were not the Lord's (5:10).

Isaiah's famous Song of the Vineyard (5:1–7) laments the fate of the people chosen by God to be a vineyard of choice vines. Because of their sins the vineyard will become a waste; *"it shall not be pruned or hoed, and it shall be overgrown with briers and thorns."* On a similar note, and with a message that prefigures the teaching of Jesus at the Last Supper, Ezekiel's Allegory of the Vine (15:1–6) forcefully reminds the people that the vine is healthy only when it produces good grapes. Without fruit the wood of the vine is fit for nothing and can only be thrown on the fire. In John, Jesus says:

I am the true vine, and my Father is the vinegrower. He
removes every branch in me that bears no fruit. Every branch
that bears fruit he prunes to make it bear more fruit. You
have already been cleansed by the word that I have spoken
to you. Abide in me as I abide in you. (15:1–4)

The Last Supper discourse weaves the vine imagery of
the Old Testament into a new pattern. The figure both
embraces the company of disciples gathered around Jesus
and stresses that he is the one who gives them life. He
keeps the community together. He enables the members to
bear fruit.

The belief that Christ is personally the binding force of
the Christian community is found in other parts of the New
Testament. We find a similar idea in Paul when he speaks
of his converts as the "body of Christ" in 1 Corinthians:
"Now you are the body of Christ, and individually members of it"
(12:27).

The reference to the Father as the one who prunes the
vine is an important element. The figure of the gardener
not only brings the allegory into line with the work of God
in the Old Testament but also strikes a note of fulfillment.
Jesus brings to completion what was promised in a way
that surpasses all expectation. He is not just another
prophet. He is the only begotten Son of God. His union
with the Father, announced in the opening verses of the
Gospel, is the reason why he can refer to himself as the true
vine. Other claimants to this status are false.

The need for pruning shows that the fruitful relationship of the branches with the vine is not automatically
guaranteed. Though the branches are meant to flourish and
bear much fruit, they can also wither, die, and be cut off.
Thus the evolving nature of the disciple's relationship to
Christ comes to the fore. Those continual acts of repentance
that characterized the old alliance are still needed; being a
branch of the vine is not a static reality.

Even if the disciples have been purified from all that
could prevent them from bearing fruit, they must make

every effort to stay united to the vine. The necessity of this reminder is underscored by the continual use of the verb "abide" in the vine discourse. The command has a forceful sense and implies adhering totally to Christ. A steadfast mutual relationship is required for the bearing of fruit. The disciples are commanded to abide in Jesus: Loyalty is the essential condition of their growth.

Discipleship demands determination. As theologian Raymond Brown comments, "Life is committed life. Therefore a branch that does not bear fruit is not simply a living, unproductive branch, but a dead branch. Some may find this interpretation harsh since it holds out no hope for the unproductive branches; yet in Johannine dualism there is not much room for an intermediate stage: there are only living and dead branches."[4]

The "Johannine dualism" mentioned by Brown is the conflict we find throughout the fourth Gospel between opposing realities—light and darkness, truth and falsehood, the Son of man and the Prince of the world. Such contrasts are characteristic of John. They have led some scholars to conclude that John's thinking was influenced by the pagan dualism prevalent in the cults flourishing at the time the Gospel was composed.

But as we have seen, the vine allegory is deeply rooted in the Old Testament. The other significant images of the fourth Gospel—bread, light, water, shepherd—can all be similarly explained; they have their origin in the writings of the prophets. The reader's attention is now drawn to the love that is a result of living in the vine:

> As the Father has loved me, so I have loved you; abide in my love. If you keep my commandments, you will abide in my love, just as I have kept my Father's commandments and abide in his love. I have said these things to you so that my joy may be in you, and that your joy may be complete. This is my commandment, that you love one another as I have loved you. No one has greater love than this, to lay down one's life for one's friends. (15:9–13)

The disciples' abiding in the vine is compared to the communion of love that has existed from all eternity in the bosom of the Father. Because of the life he draws from the Father, Jesus is the source of divine life for those who follow him.

Bearing fruit means sharing this new life with others. Through their mutual love the followers of Jesus become ever more embedded in the vine. Love between the brothers and sisters is both the fruit of union with the vine and the touchstone of Christian discipleship. This practical aspect of love brings the discourse down to earth and is a repetition of the command given at the very beginning of the Last Supper: *"I give you a new commandment, that you love one another. Just as I have loved you, you also should love one another"* (13:34).

In what way is this commandment a new one? The earlier Gospels had already spoken of loving one's neighbor and even loving one's enemies. Both Matthew's Sermon on the Mount and Luke's Sermon on the Plain make clear that the true Christian can leave nobody outside the scope of his love. The originality of the command to love in the fourth Gospel is the example of Jesus: *"As I have loved you."* Neither the synoptic nor the Pauline expressions of the love commandment make such a direct reference to the person of Christ.

The timing of the Last Supper discourse also helps us to see why the command that Jesus twice gives his followers is something new. They are to love one another in the way that he has loved his own, right up to the end. The new commandment is given at a meal, which is the final farewell before the passion, death, and return of the Son of man to the Father. These circumstances give the exhortation a particular urgency.

The example of Jesus laying down his life for his friends is the model proposed to the disciples. John solemnly states that Jesus' limitless love was the driving force that led him to lay down his life for his friends: *"Having loved his own who were in the world, he loved them to the end"* (13:1).

The practice of love establishes the disciple in the very life of God. Just as by fulfilling the Father's commandments the Son abides in his love, so the Christian, by abiding in the love of Christ, is empowered to lead a life of fruitful self-giving. The infinite embrace of the Father is the ultimate support with which the followers of Jesus live out lives of service. Their love must know no barriers and can exclude no one if they live as true children of God. *"I do not call you servants any longer, because the servant does not know what the master is doing; but I have called you friends, because I have made known to you everything that I have heard from my Father"* (15:15).

The friendship of Jesus is the gift by which he raises "his own" from the status of servants to an intimate knowledge of himself and his Father. Like Moses, to whom God spoke as a friend (Ex 33:11), the disciples enjoy the intimacy of the children of God with their Father in heaven:

> If the world hates you, be aware that it hated me before it hated you. If you belonged to the world, the world would love you as its own. Because you do not belong to the world, but I have chosen you out of the world—therefore the world hates you. (15:18–19)

The tone of the Last Supper discourse changes abruptly with these words. Up to this point Jesus has spoken of the disciples living in union with the vine and in communion with one another. Now he looks at their situation in the world. The love that the friends of Jesus are called to practice is vividly contrasted with the hatred they will have to endure from their contemporaries.

Like their master, the disciples must put up with the opposition of the unbelieving world. Jesus makes clear that such hostility is not something limited to himself. All his followers will have to bear the enmity of those who obstinately refuse to put their faith in God and the revelation of his Son.

In the intimate atmosphere of the Last Supper Jesus speaks to "his own." He reminds them that the world also loves its own. The fourth Gospel sets these two forces in opposition to each other. Here we have another example of John's dualism. The unbelieving people of the world are antagonistic to the Light. What Jesus has suffered at their hands will also happen to the disciples.

The same negative expectation of society is repeated in John's first letter : *"Do not be astonished, brothers and sisters, that the world hates you. We know that we have passed from death to life because we love one another"* (3:13–14).

Yet the ill will of their fellow citizens does not absolve the followers of Jesus from trying to win them over. The world created by God is still loved by him. If the Father so loved humanity as to send his only Son, he continues to send the followers of his Son on a mission into this darkened place of unbelief.

The members of John's community did not isolate themselves from the people among whom they lived. They did not consider themselves free to abandon their fellow citizens to the Prince of the world. In the prayer that concludes the Last Supper discourse, Jesus prays for those who are being sent into the world, just as the Father has sent him into the world, and he also prays for those who will believe through their message: *"I ask not only on behalf of these, but also on behalf of those who will believe in me through their word, that they may all be one. As you, Father, are in me and I am in you, may they also be in us"* (17:20–21).

"I Am the Bread of Life"

The promise of life, so powerfully conveyed in the image of the vine and the branches, recurs throughout John's Gospel. Two other realities of daily existence, bread and light, are used to deepen the reader's understanding of the kind of life Jesus gives to believing Christians.

John's teaching on the bread of life is concentrated in his sixth chapter. The exposition is prefaced by the multiplication of loaves for the hungry crowd that has followed Jesus into the desert. After the meal Jesus gives a speech to explain the meaning of the sign he has given.

The long bread of life discourse has been variously interpreted down through the centuries. A well-founded explanation is that in the first part (vv. 35–50) Jesus is speaking of the divine revelation he has brought to the world. In this sense the bread that Jesus gives is his spiritual teaching.

The second part of the discourse (vv. 51–58) goes on to identify the bread of life with the flesh of Jesus. The Son of man not only gives his disciples a doctrine; he also gives them himself. He is the food that brings a person to everlasting life. In the final part of the discourse the bread of life has become a figurative way of referring to the Eucharist: *"I am the bread of life. Whoever comes to me will never be hungry, and whoever believes in me will never be thirsty"* (6:35).

The first sentence of the disquisition on the bread of life, like the miracle of feeding in the desert that opens the chapter, takes us back to the Old Testament. In the Book of Sirach, wisdom declares: *"Those who eat of me will hunger for more, and those who drink of me will thirst for more"* (24:21). Sirach is saying that one can never have too much divine wisdom but will always long for more. In a similar way, Jesus proclaims that once people have grasped the revelation that he gives, they will never need any other kind of teaching.

The gift of wisdom, then, is what is offered in the first part of the discourse on the bread of life. The Old Testament background to the image would have helped the first Christian readers of the Gospel to understand what he was saying. In the Bible, eating and drinking at the messianic banquet prophesied by Isaiah (65:11–13) were traditional ways of describing the joys of the final revelation.

The synoptic Gospels regularly use the language of feasting to conjure up the delights of the final days. In Matthew 8:11, Jesus promises that many will come from the east and the west to take their places in the kingdom of heaven. In John, however, the banquet has begun. Already in his earthly existence the Son of man is the host among those who have been invited.

After Jesus feeds the multitude with a miraculous multiplication of loaves, in response to the demand for more bread he declares that he is the bread of life. He formally offers the nourishment of divine wisdom to those who believe in him. The only fitting response to this revelation is faith. In this first part of the discourse the evangelist is reminding us of the need to accept the teaching of Jesus.

"I am the living bread that came down from heaven. Whoever eats of this bread will live forever; and the bread that I will give for the life of the world is my flesh" (6:51). The second part of the bread of life discourse concentrates on the eucharistic dimension of the gift that Jesus offers. This sacramental aspect forms the climax to chapter 6. Earlier, in chapter 4, Jesus had spoken of giving living water but he did not identify himself as living water. Now he declares categorically that he is the bread of life. The disciple is called not only to believe but also to eat and to drink.

In speaking of the bread as his flesh, Jesus adds that it has come down from heaven. We are reminded of the prologue where the entrance of the Word into the world was spoken of in terms of becoming flesh (1:14). The same flesh is now offered to men and women as living bread: *"Those who eat my flesh and drink my blood abide in me, and I in them"* (6:56).

The promise of close communion with Jesus through eating the bread of life is similar to what he says in the allegory of the vine. The Eucharist is one of the principal ways to nourish the disciple's union with Christ. Even though John, unlike the synoptists, does not record the institution of the Eucharist at the Last Supper, he stresses the necessity of receiving the sacrament for the spiritual growth of the Christian. To eat the flesh of the Son of man implies, already in this world, a deep relationship with Christ. But there is even more: The bread that has come down from heaven is the means by which the faithful also enter, through their union with the Son, into communion with the Father.

In this second part of the bread of life discourse, Jesus speaks of his "flesh" (*sarx*) and not of his "body" (*soma*). The latter is the word used in the synoptic accounts of the institution of the Eucharist. John's choice of terms brings out the realism of the offer. At the same time, while the fourth Gospel insists on the reality of the eucharistic flesh and blood, there is no question of a merely automatic reception of the sacrament being fruitful for eternal life.

With its stress on believing the words of Jesus, the first part of the discourse has made clear that there is no magical operation of divine blessing. When eternal life is promised to those who partake of the flesh of the Son of man in the second part, the need for faith is already firmly established. Taken together, the two parts on the bread of life lead the reader to the necessary conclusion—the eucharistic flesh of Jesus, to be truly life-giving, must be received with deep faith.

"Because of this many of his disciples turned back and no longer went about with him" (6:66). The response of many disciples to the bread of life pronouncement is unbelief. The rejection of Jesus by his own people at Nazareth, narrated in Luke, is paralleled in the conclusion of John's sixth chapter. Just as the synoptic account of the ministry in Galilee ended in disbelief, so at the end of the teaching on the bread of life many no longer "walk" with him. Jesus will meet the same fate in Jerusalem, where the majority of the people will not accept him.

The reaction of unbelief and the decision not to follow Jesus also fit into the Old Testament background to the bread of life instruction. The invitations of wisdom to come and eat (Sir 24:19–20) are not accepted by everybody. There are always those foolish enough to reject the way of spiritual knowledge and turn from the path that God opens before them.

The bread of life teaching is the occasion of misunderstanding and finally division. Like the allegory of the vine and the branches, John's sixth chapter leaves the reader in no doubt that there are conditions attached to Christian discipleship. Continuing commitment is not a foregone conclusion. The departure of so many after the teaching shows that the following of Christ, although meant to grow and deepen, can also deteriorate and even die.

The on-going dimension of discipleship is also a salient feature of John's belief that Jesus is the light of the world. To this we now turn to complement the "I am" saying on the bread of life and the allegory of the vine.

"I Am the Light of the World"

The synoptists use the imagery of a lamp to describe the good news that Jesus has brought. The lamp of the gospel should not be hidden away but must be put in a prominent place so that it can illuminate the whole house (Lk 11:33). In the fourth Gospel the symbol of light becomes one more way the evangelist pivots his message on the person of Christ. Jesus has not merely brought a lamp into the world. He is the lamp that gives light of the world: *"I am the light of the world. Whoever follows me will never walk in darkness, but will have the light of life"* (8:12).

The disciples are told in Matthew 5:14 that they are to give light to those around them. The fourth Gospel leaves them in no doubt that they can give effective witness only insofar as they reflect the light of Christ.

We have seen that the Old Testament provides the background to John's figurative use of the vine and the bread of life. The same holds true for the image of light. In a well-known prediction, Isaiah foretold that a light would dawn in the region of Galilee: *"The people who walked in darkness have seen a great light; those who lived in a land of deep darkness—on them light has shined"* (9:2). Isaiah repeated the promise when speaking of the call of the mysterious suffering servant of God. This servant would be a *"light to the nations"* (42:6).

Jesus' action in the cure of a man born blind, narrated in chapter 9, is a pointer in this direction: His divine commission is verified by his ability to open the eyes of the blind. Through curing the blind man Jesus shows he has the right to be considered the light of the world. He fulfills the promise of healing associated with the One who is to bring light into the darkened universe.

"Whoever follows me will never walk in darkness." The clear-cut option between walking in the darkness or walking in the light illustrates the moral stance of the fourth Gospel. We are either in the light or in the darkness. There are no gray areas in John. The evangelist provides us with no fences on which to sit. The choice between the light and the darkness is unqualified. There is no third way.

Again we have an example of the oppositions that are found in the fourth Gospel. John's absolute distinction between light and darkness has prompted speculation that his language is rooted in the non-Christian religions of the period. They also spoke of light and darkness as products of two opposing principles of creation, one good the other evil.

Yet the division between light and darkness can be found in the earliest parts of the Old Testament and we do not need to go to pagan cults to find the contrast. The Book of Genesis described the creation of light and darkness. The psalmist spoke of the light that gives life in Psalm 56:13, for example. Most importantly, in the Old Testament both light and darkness were firmly placed under the control of the Creator. They were never depicted as two independent principles of good and evil.

There have been few societies in the course of history that have not used the contrast between light and darkness to signify the conflict between good and evil. "This is an archetypal symbol, rooted in the deepest instinct of the human race."[5] The chord is already sounded in the opening bars of the fourth Gospel:

> All things came into being through him, and without him not one thing came into being. What has come into being in him was life, and the life was the light of all people. The light shines in the darkness, and the darkness did not overcome it. (1:35)

The hymn to the divine Word, which forms the opening eighteen verses of John's Gospel, is considered the supreme composition of the evangelist. The prologue is a fitting preface to the continual emphasis on the divine personality of Jesus found on every page of the Gospel. If the eagle is the symbol of John, this tribute is due in major part to the lofty flight of the prologue.

In a manner reminiscent of Paul's hymn in Philippians 2:6–11, the prologue begins by stating that the Word is divine. But whereas Paul speaks of Jesus emptying himself, being born in the likeness of human beings and taking on the form of a slave, the prologue simply states that *"the Word became flesh."* Paul's hymn ends with Jesus exalted and proclaimed by every tongue as Lord, to the glory of God the Father. The final verse of the prologue states that the only Son is in the bosom of the Father.

The drama of salvation, presented elsewhere in the fourth Gospel as a conflict between the Son of man and the Prince of this world, is described in the prologue as a struggle between light and darkness. Though good in origin, the created order has fallen under the spell of moral evil and is now a place of darkness where sin holds sway.

Yet, despite being enshrouded in darkness and error, the human race is still loved by God. As a sign of his great love God has sent a ray of divine light, his only begotten Son, into the world. At least where he is present, Jesus dispels the shadows of iniquity. A firm belief in God's benevolence towards men and women together with the conviction that they are in a state of moral disorder are the twin components of John's worldview.

Similar to the First Letter of John, which states that God is light with no admixture of darkness (1:5), the prologue identifies Jesus as the light. He has come into the world to dispel the darkness of wrongdoing. The fall of the human race described at the beginning of Genesis, though not mentioned explicitly in the fourth Gospel, is presupposed. The consoling message of the prologue is that those who believe in the One who has come from God will not remain in the deep night of impiety.

John starts from the basic premise that the Word alone can give light and life to the human race. The Word is not an abstract notion but a divine person who has become flesh in Jesus Christ. The link between the creation of the world and the mission of Jesus clarifies as the Gospel unfolds. The life-giving power of the Word, which was intended for the whole human race, has become a reality for those who believe in Jesus. Despite the skepticism of people such as Nathaniel, something good, something astonishingly wonderful has come out of Nazareth (1:46).

The promise of life, central to John's writing, replaces the coming kingdom of God, so dear to Matthew, Mark, and Luke in the proclamation of the gospel. Yet the two interpretations of the good news are not as far apart as they may seem. In the fourth Gospel the disciples are promised a particular kind of life. John distinguishes two forms of existence. There is ordinary, earthly life (*bios*) and there is eternal life (*zoe*). The possibility Christ offers to those who believe in him is *zoe*, eternal life. This eternal life has already begun for those who accept the word of Jesus and follow him.

Consequently, when Jesus says he has come to give life, and give life to the full (10:10), the meaning of this oft-quoted and sometimes misquoted text is not merely human growth or earthly fulfillment. What is offered to the disciple is much more: A share of the divine Spirit who is an inexhaustible source of grace for those who walk in the light.

The concepts of light and life thus form a closely allied pair in John's vision. Life, however, is the more basic notion and for this reason life is the central metaphor of the fourth Gospel. Light is an image showing the divine life under a particular aspect. Light is the illumination that the Word has been giving to the world from the beginning of creation. The revealing action of the Word reaches its climax in the incarnation, when the Word becomes flesh. By giving his followers the light of his teaching, Jesus thereby offers them the radiance of eternal life.

"We must work the works of him who sent me while it is day; night is coming when no one can work. As long as I am in the world, I am the light of the world" (9:4–5). Jesus' claim to be the light of the world and his promise of life are made concrete in the miracles he performs. Miraculous deeds are called "signs" in the fourth Gospel because they point to the true nature of Jesus.

One clear example of the power of Jesus to be the light of the world is the cure of the man born blind narrated in chapter 9. Through his extended account of the miracle, which takes up the whole of the chapter, the evangelist depicts the way Jesus can give life and unmask what is hidden in the human heart. The confrontation with the unbelieving Jews, which the sign provokes, is the occasion to penetrate further into the mystery of the One who is the light of the world.[6]

Chapter 9 recounts how a man who once lived in darkness was brought into the light, not only through a physical cure, but above all through the inner enlightenment of faith. Though there are stories of the blind being cured in the synoptists, the singularity of John's account is the fullness of the discussion that succeeds the miracle. The evangelist uses the cure to illustrate his presentation of Jesus as the life-giving light of the world.

No other miracle in the fourth Gospel is narrated with so much detail and even humor, especially in the way the cured man deals with the persistent questions of the Pharisees. These particulars serve to clarify what is going on between Jesus, the cured man, and the Pharisees. While the former blind man is gradually moving into the brightness of faith, the Pharisees, who resist the sign, plunge further and further into the shadows of unbelief.

John gives a highly dramatic thrust to the narrative, making the story serve his purpose and clarify his teaching from two different angles. The chapter begins with a blind man who is about to be cured by Jesus. It ends with the man's confession of faith. In sharp contrast, the Pharisees refuse to accept his testimony about Jesus. As he gains sight and insight, they become spiritually blind.

The actual healing of the blind man with spittle reminds us of a similar action recounted by Mark (8:23). However, in John's chapter 9 the events following the cure are the real focus of the narrative. Throughout his interrogation by the Pharisees, the former blind man displays a deepening faith in Jesus. Slowly but surely he comes into the light. First of all he refers to *"the man they call Jesus."* Then, under scrutiny from the Pharisees, he proclaims that Jesus is *a prophet* (v. 17). In the final dialogue with the Pharisees he professes Jesus to be a man *who has come from God* (v. 33). The climax of the account is the meeting of Jesus with the man who was formerly blind. He is worshiped and professed to be *the Son of man* (v. 37).

The Pharisees, on the other hand, become more and more resistant to the truth. During their first interrogation they seem to accept the fact of the healing. They discuss among themselves whether Jesus, in view of the sign he has given, could be a man from God, despite his breach of the Sabbath law. At the second interview, a more hostile view prevails and even the miracle is put under suspicion. The Pharisees try to show through the testimony of the man's parents that he was not really blind in the first place.

In the last interrogation the Pharisees seek to trap the man by having him contradict himself (v. 26). Nothing will now convince them to become followers of Jesus. They are disciples of Moses *"but as for this man, we do not know where he comes from"* (6:29). They attack the cured man and throw him out. Thus the Pharisees who sat in judgment are judged guilty themselves. They fulfill the prophecy of Jesus: *"I came into the world for judgment so that those who do not see may see, and those who do see may become blind"* (6:39).

The cure of the man born blind is a commentary in action on the claim of Jesus to be the light of the world. Like the Old Testament prophets who accompanied their preaching with colorful illustrations and mighty deeds, Jesus too proves that he can make good the promise that those who follow him will have the light of life (8:12). His power triumphs over the darkness that pervades the earth.

His goodness bears the radiance of eternal glory to those who are prepared to open themselves to his presence in faith. Through the signs that he gives and the invitation he offers Jesus brings the blind not only to sight but also to discipleship.[7]

Reflections

The fourth Gospel depicts the personal relationship between the disciple and Jesus in different ways. The Christian is called to live as a member of the vine, be nourished with the bread of life, and view all created reality in the brightness of faith that radiates from Christ, the light of the world.

Yet the very emphasis with which John presents the personal call to faith has led some writers to conclude that the evangelist is not concerned with the need for community. What has been called the "individualism" of the fourth Gospel seems to forget about the ecclesial nature of Christian discipleship.

As we read through the bread of life discourse we do notice that the stress is on the individual disciple's union with Christ: *"Those who eat my flesh and drink my blood have eternal life, and I will raise them up on the last day"* (6:54). If we compare this with Paul's eucharistic teaching, we find a different approach. In his First Letter to the Corinthians, Paul is concerned with the community and its manner of celebrating the Eucharist.

At the same time, the social dimension of the Eucharist is not entirely absent from the fourth Gospel. In this regard, the breakfast scene in the last chapter of John (21:9–14) has a special significance. There is a certain eucharistic symbolism in the meal provided by the risen Christ for the disciples after their night of fishing. The words of distribution have a clear echo of the eucharistic institution: *"Jesus came and took the bread and gave it to them, and did the same with the fish"* (21:13). The encounter points to the meal with the risen Lord as the center of community life and a privileged sign of union with the risen Lord. The Eucharist was not a purely individual celebration in John's community.[8]

We have also seen that ancient Israel forms the most likely background to the symbols of the vine, the bread of life, and the light of the world. "The people of God" in the Old Testament is the crucial starting point that, once accepted, weakens any interpretation of John that reduces his message to an isolated call having no concern for a community as such.

The allegory of the vine, in particular, rules out the possibility of a disciple living an independent, solitary existence. The Father is the gardener who has planted the vine and prunes the branches. The disciples are to bear fruit for his glory (15:8). On a tree the living branches are not only united to the trunk; they are also joined to one another. An isolated branch not somehow linked to the rest of the tree will not bear fruit. So the vine image, by its nature, points to the unity between Jesus and the community and to the bond that exists among the disciples themselves. For this reason the discourse on the vine and the branches is often considered the counterpart to Paul's doctrine of the church as the body of Christ.

Jesus' priestly prayer for his disciples at the end of the Last Supper should also be taken as referring to a group of believers. They are the ones whom the Father has given to the special care of Jesus: *"I have made your name known to those whom you gave me from the world. They were yours, and you gave them to me, and they have kept your word"* (17:6).

We can take John's concern for unity a step further. The evangelist was not preoccupied solely with his own particular community, oblivious of the wider mission of the church. He did not stand in isolation from the greater Christian community of the day, unconcerned about the salvation of those who lived in the darkness of the world. A missionary thrust is present right through the fourth Gospel, starting with the coming of Jesus from the Father to bring the light of life.

The chief reason why the community dimension is not more evident in the fourth Gospel is the stress on Christ that dominates every consideration. John's profound vision of the Son of God subsumes all other elements of the Gospel.

When John's church became entangled in the internal struggles reflected in his letters, there may have been a desire to forge closer links with the greater Christian community. If this is what happened, the whole church was able to benefit from the meditations of the Johannine circle. At the same time, the adherents of this circle, notwithstanding their brilliance, accepted that they had not covered every aspect of Christian doctrine. There were other aspects of the faith that needed to be kept in mind to complement their almost exclusive concentration on the divine nature of Jesus. The second conclusion to the Gospel indicates such awareness: *"But there are also many other things that Jesus did; if every one of them were written down, I suppose that the world itself could not contain the books that would be written"* (21:25).

SIX

Priests and Presbyters

Hebrews, 1 Peter, and the Pastoral Letters

B efore examining the manner in which the New Testament speaks of priests, one fact needs to be stated. During his earthly life Jesus of Nazareth was not regarded as a priest. He was a layman. Although he had dealings with the different authorities in Jerusalem, including the priestly rulers, he had no official position or power base there. He did not possess the essential requirement of the priesthood in his own society—membership in the tribe of Levi.

The infancy narratives of Matthew and Luke report and even stress that Jesus was born of the house of David. He was considered to be the son of Joseph. From Joseph he inherited his legal status as a member of David's clan. Consequently Jesus was not born into one of the Levitical families, which alone had the right to offer worship in the Temple: *"Now the one of whom these things are spoken belonged to another tribe, from which no one has ever served at the altar"* (Heb 7:13).

As we shall see, the author of the Epistle to the Hebrews says that Jesus became a priest by his sacrificial death on the cross and entry into heaven. Enthroned as high priest, he intercedes for us at the right hand of the Father. Only through this heavenly intercession and not because of his earthly status can Jesus be considered a priest: *"Now if he were on earth, he would not be a priest at all . . ."* (Heb 8:4).

Jesus was born a Jewish layperson, lived out his life as a Jewish layperson, and died a Jewish layperson. Indeed, his relationships with the priests in Jerusalem are recorded in the Gospels as hostile. This probably reflects Jesus' actual historical relationship with the priesthood of his day.

The Letter to the Hebrews

A wag once said, there are only three things certain about the Letter of St. Paul to the Hebrews: It was not written by St. Paul; it was not written to the Hebrews; and it is not a letter! Most modern scholarship would support the witticism.

The attribution of Hebrews to St. Paul dates back to the second century. Two of the greatest patristic writers, Augustine and Jerome, accepted the Pauline authorship. As a result, Hebrews was counted among the fourteen Epistles of St. Paul at the Council of Carthage in 419.

But the elaborate style and the particular message of Hebrews rule out Pauline authorship. Paul's favorite expression, "Christ Jesus," never appears in the text. More importantly, the big issue for Paul, the resurrection of Jesus, is only mentioned once in Hebrews. Though there have been many attempts to find out the identity of the person who refers to "our brother Timothy" in 13:23, these guesses remain completely in the realm of speculation. All we can say with probability is that the author was a second-generation Christian who wrote sometime between A.D. 60 and 90.

The title "to the Hebrews" does not appear in the text but was a deduction of early commentators. The designation was in common use by the end of the second century, although whom "the Hebrews" precisely meant is now difficult to ascertain. Different Christian communities are thought to have been the recipients of the Epistle. Rome seems the most likely destination and in fact the imperial capital was the first place to acknowledge the existence of the work, as can be seen in the first-century letter of Clement of Rome.

The Christians in Rome were of Jewish origin and may have retained a loyalty to the Jerusalem Temple. The Epistle would then have a definite purpose: To remind them that the new covenant had made the former one and its sacrificial practices obsolete. What counted now was the heavenly priesthood of Christ.

The author presents his work as a "word of exhortation" (13:22). This would indicate a sermon of some kind as can be seen from Acts 13:15 where Paul and Barnabas, asked if they have a word of encouragement for the people, respond with a homily to the assembly.

> Long ago God spoke to our ancestors in many and various ways by the prophets, but in these last days he has spoken to us by a Son, whom he appointed heir of all things, through whom he also created the worlds. He is the reflection of God's glory and the exact imprint of God's very being, and he sustains all things by his powerful word. When he had made purification for sins, he sat down at the right hand of the Majesty on high, having become as much superior to angels as the name he has inherited is more excellent than theirs. (Heb 1:1–4)

The four opening verses of Hebrews focus our attention on the one through whom God speaks to the world. In the body of the work Jesus receives a number of titles: Son, mediator, shepherd of the sheep and, most significant of all, great high priest. The treatise is an exhortation to Christian living based on the person and mission of Jesus.

The author presumes reader or listener acquaintance with the story of Jesus of Nazareth and does not elaborate any historical details of his life, except for the central facts of the passion and death. With no references to the earthly ministry and teaching of Jesus, the letter directs the reader's attention to his heavenly dignity and intercession.

For the author of Hebrews, a priest is essentially a mediator between the human race and the divine Creator. He is a bridge-builder (*pontifex*) between God and his people. So to fulfill his role as the great high priest Jesus must be in relationship with both God and the people he is going to represent before the throne of mercy. The opening chapters of Hebrews are dedicated to describing both these aspects of Jesus' life.

On the one hand, he is the Son of God, superior to the angels and the ministers of the Old Testament liturgy. He brings to perfection all that was good and holy in the first covenant. On the other hand, the author insists that Jesus is like us in everything, sin excluded. He was capable of suffering and he bore our trials and infirmities. He knew what it was to be tested by God. He was not ashamed to call us his brothers and sisters (2:11).

To show the superiority of Christ's priesthood over that of the Old Testament, Hebrews says that the first covenant was not capable of establishing a full relationship between God and the human race. As a result, the liturgy of the Temple stressed the separation between God and us. The offerings of the Levitical priests were unable to purify men and women and bring them into real communion with God. The Levitical priesthood, by its very nature, was imperfect and provisional.

To remedy the deficiencies of the ancient cult, God promised a new covenant. This would not be something external, but would be inscribed in the depths of the heart. To achieve this end God commissioned his Son as the new high priest. He did not enter the sanctuary of heaven by means of the blood of animals, but *"with his own blood, thus obtaining eternal redemption"* (9:12).

There are isolated texts in other works of the New Testament that speak of Christ and his death on the cross in terms of the priesthood. In Romans 3:25 Paul says that God presented Jesus as a sacrifice of atonement. In what is called "the high priestly prayer" of the fourth Gospel Jesus announces: *"I sanctify myself, so that they also may be sanctified in truth"* (Jn 17:19).

The fourth Gospel says that the risen body of Jesus replaces the Temple sanctuary (2:21). According to John, Jesus was condemned to death as a sacrificial lamb at the moment the lambs were being prepared for the Passover sacrifice. Some commentators believe that the description of the tunic stripped from Jesus before he died is a reference to the tunic of the Jewish high priest.[1]

Yet, even though these hints can be found in other parts of the New Testament, in Hebrews the high priesthood of Jesus is the major theme. He is presented first and foremost as the high priest who effectively abolishes the old Levitical sacrifices. Jesus is a priest according to the order of Melchizedek. Here too the Letter to the Hebrews is quite distinctive in its teaching:

> So also Christ did not glorify himself in becoming a high priest, but was appointed by the one who said to him, "You are my Son, today I have begotten you": as he says also in another place, "You are a priest forever, according to the order of Melchizedek."
>
> In the days of his flesh, Jesus offered up prayers and supplications, with loud cries and tears, to the one who was able to save him from death, and he was heard because of his reverent submission. Although he was a Son, he learned obedience through what he suffered; and having been made perfect, he became the source of eternal salvation for all who obey him, having been designated by God a high priest according to the order of Melchizedek. (5:5–10)

This key text in Hebrews explains how Jesus became a high priest in three great steps: He was chosen by God for the role; he proved his fidelity in suffering; and his prayer on the cross was heard by God and thus he became the source of salvation for all people.

First, the author says that Jesus was chosen by the direct pronouncement of the Father. He did not seek the glory of the priesthood but had it thrust upon him. Chosen from his brothers and sisters, Jesus also possessed the other dimension of mediation necessary to be a true priest—

union with God. He is in fact the eternal Son whose dignity ranks higher than that of the angels. Therefore he possessed in a manner impossible for ordinary mortals the qualities of a true priest. Jesus is the supreme bridge builder between God and the created world.

Second, despite the glory of being chosen for the priesthood, or rather by the very fact of that choice, the way followed by Jesus was one of suffering, supplicant prayer, and obedience. We have here a reference to the passion. Calvary was the altar of sacrifice upon which Christ offered himself. He did this to gain pardon for a sinful world.

Third, the fidelity of Jesus in the days of his flesh—that is to say, during the weakness of his mortal life—reached its climax at the time of his agonized prayer to the One who could save him from death. We are reminded of Mark's account of the passion. During his agony in the garden Jesus begged his Father to remove the cup of suffering and on the cross he cried out in dereliction: *"My God, my God why have you forsaken me?"* (15:34).

The death of Jesus is seen in Hebrews as a prayer offered on our behalf by the great high priest. Jesus learned what being fully human meant through suffering. Son though he was, he too had to be tested in the crucible of obedience. Though he was without sin (4:15), he did not escape the lot of every person born into this world. Such an apprenticeship was essential if he was to be the true mediator. He not only had a share in the divine nature; he also had to accept the human condition to its fullest in order to become the supreme mediator between God and his people.

The dignity of the high priesthood was therefore the outcome of his fidelity. He had shown himself capable of enduring all that life could throw at him and still retain his attentive and loving obedience to the Father. Raised to the priestly office by his passion, Jesus *"is able for all time to save those who approach God through him, since he always lives to make intercession for them"* (7:25).

After being perfected through his obedience he went before us into the heavenly sanctuary as the pioneer of our salvation. The mediation of the high priest on behalf of his disciples is the consequence of the ascension of Jesus into the glory of heaven. There he sits at the right hand of God. The essential benefit we derive from the priestly consecration of Jesus is the assurance of his heavenly intercession. The once-and-for-all sacrifice of Jesus on Calvary, which is how Hebrews interprets the death on the cross, is prolonged in heaven by the prayer of our great high priest before the throne of God.

Jesus is a priest according to the order of Melchizedek. The author uses this comparison to show that, unlike the Levitical priests of the Old Testament, the priesthood of Jesus is eternal. The mysterious figure of the priest of Salem, who made an offering of bread and wine on behalf of Abraham (Gen 14:17–24), did not belong to the Levitical priesthood. No one knows anything about his lineage or where he came from. Melchizedek suddenly appeared on the scene and just as quickly disappeared, leaving no trace behind. Because of the mystery surrounding him, the priest of Salem is seen by the author of Hebrews as foreshadowing Christ, whose origins are also lost in mystery and whose priesthood is superior to that of the Levites.

The perfect offering of the true high priest means that the Temple ceremonies of the old law have lost their reason for existence. The author goes on to develop this point in the body of his work. The Temple liturgy was incapable of achieving its end, despite the frequent oblations of the priests. Indeed, the very frequency of the rituals stemmed from the total inability of animal sacrifices to make an offering truly pleasing to God.

The new covenant has been able to achieve this purpose. The priesthood of Christ reaches across the deep divide between God and us. In his person, through his priesthood, Jesus offers his disciples the bridge along which they can walk with full assurance into the presence of the living God. The sacrifice of the cross has ended the need for ritual separation:

> Therefore, my friends, since we have confidence to enter the
> sanctuary by the blood of Jesus, by the new and living way
> that he opened for us through the curtain (that is, through
> his flesh), and since we have a great priest over the house of
> God, let us approach with a true heart in full assurance of
> faith, with our hearts sprinkled clean from an evil conscience
> and our bodies washed with pure water. Let us hold fast to
> the confession of our hope without wavering, for he who has
> promised is faithful. And let us consider how to provoke one
> another to love and good deeds, not neglecting to meet
> together, as is the habit of some, but encouraging one
> another, and all the more as you see the Day approaching.
> (10:19–25)

The confidence of Christ's disciples to enter the presence of God is the practical outcome of Jesus' fidelity on the cross. In view of what has been accomplished for us by our great high priest, we can approach the throne of God with boldness.

Such confidence is the birthright of Christians and is the opposite of the fear of the divine presence that was prevalent in the old dispensation. The Jewish high priest was limited to a yearly performance of the sacred rites and was subjected to severe restrictions. Even on the feast of Atonement he did not prolong his prayer in the Holy of Holies lest the people become frightened. In direct contrast, the disciples of Christ have no need to fear the holy place. Because the blood of Jesus has purified them they can enter without trepidation.

The passion of Jesus has inaugurated a new way into the presence of God. His physical death was an action that lifted the curtain separating us from the divine presence. The synoptic Gospels make the same point when they speak, as does Mark in 15:38, of the Temple veil being rent in two at the moment of Jesus' death. The rending of the Temple veil is an event of deep symbolic meaning.

Let us draw near to God, then, the author urges his readers. No longer is the privilege of access to him constricted by the limitations surrounding the high priest when he made his annual entry into the Holy of Holies on the Day of Atonement. At the same time, the writer reminds us, there are certain conditions to fulfill if the followers of Jesus are to reap the full benefits of his priestly mediation: They must practice the virtues of faith, hope, and love.

Like St. Paul, the author of Hebrews sees the Christian life as rooted in faith. The whole tenor of the Epistle shows the incapacity of the cultic prescriptions of the Old Testament to justify a person in the sight of God. Mere human effort cannot serve as the basis of salvation; faith in the divine mediator is the first requirement for a life of union with God. Such faith is more than an intellectual assent to the doctrine of salvation. The disciple must imitate Jesus' trusting disposition. Despite his trials, he never lost confidence in the One who could save him from death.

Christian love and the performance of good deeds (*"beautiful works"* in the original text) are the ultimate fruits of union with the compassionate high priest who has given his life for us. The mutual love of the disciples will show itself in a practical manner by assisting those in need and by encouraging one another to be faithful to the gatherings of the congregation. (These latter probably mean the assembly of the community for worship. This would fit in perfectly with the baptismal reference of *"our bodies washed with pure water"*).

The Epistle to the Hebrews therefore concludes its treatment of the priesthood of Christ by showing how Christians have the right to approach the throne of God with confidence. Provided they come in faith, hope, and love, they can enter the divine presence. By reason of their baptism, they are in fact a "priestly people," though the author never uses this phrase in describing them. For such a designation we must turn to two other works of the New Testament: 1 Peter and the Book of Revelation.

The Royal Priesthood

The First Letter of Peter looks at the Christian life in a way that is greatly influenced by the Old Testament. This is most clearly seen in the kind of language the author uses. For example, he compares the precious blood of Christ to *"that of a lamb without defect or blemish"* (1:18–19). We have here a reference to the paschal lamb of Exodus.

The Letter compares the pilgrimage of faith to the most significant events of the Old Testament—the Exodus, the desert wandering, and entry into the Promised Land. The followers of Jesus are described as enduring a time of exile while they wait for the incorruptible inheritance of heaven (1:4). Just as the Jewish people were urged to gird up their loins and get ready for a quick departure from Egypt, so the recipients of the Letter are exhorted to gird up their minds (1:13). Like the people of the old covenant, they are given the divine command, *"You shall be holy, for I am holy"* (1:15–16).

The influence of the Jewish heritage on Christianity has to be borne in mind when interpreting the writer's thoughts on the royal priesthood.

Come to him, a living stone though rejected by mortals yet chosen and precious in God's sight, and like living stones, let yourselves be built into a spiritual house, to be a holy priesthood, to offer spiritual sacrifices acceptable to God through Jesus Christ. For it stands in scripture: "See, I am laying in Zion a stone, a cornerstone chosen and precious; and whoever believes in him will not be put to shame."

To you then who believe, he is precious; but for those who do not believe, "The stone that the builders rejected has become the very head of the corner," and "A stone that makes them stumble, and a rock that makes them fall." They stumble because they disobey the word, as they were destined to do.

But you are a chosen race, a royal priesthood, a holy nation, God's own people, in order that you may proclaim the mighty acts of him who called you out of darkness into his marvelous light. Once you were not a people, but now you are God's people; once you had not received mercy, but now you have received mercy. (1 Pet 2:4–10)

These seven verses form one of the most substantial descriptions of the Christian life in the entire New Testament. The whole passage is a complex interlocking of biblical quotations and images "stitched together like a vivid patchwork quilt that presents a stunning image of the church."[2]

First of all, Christians are "living stones." Laid on the foundation that is Christ, the stone rejected by men but chosen by God, the followers of Jesus are built into a spiritual house. They are told to place their confidence in him who, though spurned by unbelievers, has been raised up by God to be the living cornerstone. The active love required of the living stones means that they do not form a static building. The disciples of Christ are not an isolated group on the fringes of society; they are not withdrawn from the world.

The sacred building formed by such living stones is no longer a material temple, but a living community where God is present and in which he receives true worship. The Jerusalem Temple was a central institution of Jewish life. Now 1 Peter uses the language of that sacred place to describe the presence of Christ and the community gathered around him. To be part of such a sacred place requires holiness and those works of service that become spiritual sacrifices acceptable to God.

The building up of the community is an on-going process. Yet not all who are invited to become part of the building react constructively. The person of Jesus is a rock standing squarely in the flow of human history and deciding the destiny of those who encounter him. The people who base their lives on his teaching and put their trust in him *"will not be put to shame."* The ones who do not cling to this rock of salvation *"stumble because they disobey the word."*

The author uses a variety of Old Testament images to demonstrate the dynamic nature of the invitation to come to Christ, the living stone. He incorporates a number of images to describe what it means to belong to the community. Thus the disciples of Jesus, by responding positively, are a "chosen race," "a royal priesthood," "a holy nation," "God's own people."

The author searches through the Old Testament to find symbols and concepts that can describe what it means to belong to the church of Christ. The most helpful of all is the covenant. Through their election and the holiness of their lives, Christians have entered a new covenant with God.

Closely associated with the idea of covenant is the description of the disciples as a "royal priesthood." We find the same combination of themes in the Book of Exodus. When God offered to make a covenant with Israel he promised, *"Now therefore, if you obey my voice and keep my covenant, you shall be my treasured possession out of all the peoples. Indeed, the whole earth is mine, but you shall be for me a priestly kingdom and a holy nation"* (Ex 19:5–6).

This promise is the background for understanding the term "royal priesthood" used by the author of 1 Peter. Through their election by God and holiness of life, Christians participate in the privileged status of the royal priesthood. In other words, they enjoy a special relationship with God. As a body, as a people, they are given the mission to proclaim his holiness throughout the world.

However, we have to remember that in the Old Testament the royal priesthood of the people was not seen in any way as opposed to the cultic ministry exercised by the Levitical priests. There is no evidence that the text of Exodus was ever employed in a polemical way against the Temple priesthood. The institution of a sacrificing order of priests in Israel was quite distinctive and preserved its unique status right up to the destruction of the Temple in A.D. 70.

Therefore to see the text of Exodus as opposing the Levitical priesthood of the Old Testament is to go against the rest of the biblical evidence. The prophets, of course, often denounced the sacrifices of the people because they were performed without sincerity of heart. But the internal organization of the community's worship was never in question.

God himself protected and guaranteed the service of the Levitical priesthood. Thus when Korah challenged Moses and the priests by proclaiming *"all the congregation are holy, every one of them,"* he was punished with divine retribution (Num 16:1–35). There is no reason, then, to suppose that the mention of a royal priesthood in Exodus was made in opposition to the ministerial priesthood of the Old Testament.

Interpreting the text of 1 Peter on the "royal priesthood" in the same way as the Old Testament used the expression, we see that the term has a figurative meaning. It is not used in the strict sense of cultic ministry exercised by the Levitical priesthood but denotes the believing community as the elect People of God. The wonderful vocation the people received from God at Sinai is now, says the author of 1 Peter, the privilege of the followers of Christ. As a community they too have been elected to be a royal priesthood and a holy nation.

Election for mission, not worship at the altar, is the keynote of the "royal priesthood." The disciples of Christ have been chosen for a special purpose. Like the ancient Jews scattered throughout the world, their mission is to give witness to the holiness of God among the pagan peoples with whom they live.

Martin Luther appealed to 1 Peter for his interpretation of the general priesthood of the faithful during the sixteenth-century Protestant Reformation. Through baptism, he said, every believer has been made a priest. He used the text of 1 Peter to support his attack on the ordained ministry of the day. This rejection of the ministerial priesthood became one of the reasons for the ultimate break with Catholicism.

In recent times there has been a shift to a more ecumenical approach. A modern Protestant commentary on the text points in the new direction:

When the passage of 1 Peter is analyzed, on the other hand, within its own first-century literary and historical setting, it reveals a rather different meaning. In this original context it is election (of Jesus Christ and his community) rather than priesthood which is principally stressed. A priesthood theme, in fact, is nowhere mentioned in the rest of the letter, in contrast to the dominant theme of election. Moreover, this passage affirms not the equality of all believers as individual priests or kings but rather cites collective terms (generation, dwelling place, household, priestly community, nation, people) to emphasize the community and divine favor of the new covenant people of God.[3]

1 Peter uses another phrase to bring out the community's sense of being chosen: They are a "holy nation." Though God's elect have different ethnic origins, their shared vocation as Christians breaks through the barriers of culture and race and gives them a sense of common identity. Because God has called them all, they too are sacred. This holiness does not mean withdrawal from the pagan world but, on the contrary, is a grace for the benefit of the other nations. They form a community with the worldwide mission of giving witness to the all-holy God.

The final appellation of the passage in 1 Peter, *"the people of God,"* neatly sums up the chosen status of Christ's disciples. Christians are God's own people. The word *people* was the term most commonly used in the Old Testament to describe Israel as the community gathered together by God. In applying this designation to the Christian community, the author recognizes the place of the disciples in God's plan and their continuity with the people of the first covenant.

The Book of Revelation is our second source for understanding the term "royal priesthood" as applied in a general way to the followers of Christ. Apart from other essential aspects that we shall consider in the next chapter, the Book of Revelation has a definite liturgical slant. This awareness can help us understand more clearly the hymns of praise found in the text. The author makes frequent references to the sanctuary and the altar; he gives descriptions of the various persons involved in worship.

Although Revelation attributes special titles to Christ, he is never called a priest. Rather he is the One who receives the worship of the heavenly court. The followers of Jesus are the people who are given the attributes of priesthood and kingdom. This is done in three different places: 1:5–6, 5:10, and 20:6.

"To him who loves us and freed us from our sins by his blood, and made us to be a kingdom, priests serving his God and Father, to him be glory and dominion forever and ever. Amen" (1:5-6). These solemn words of praise and homage are found at the beginning of Revelation. The author considers the final result of Jesus' self-offering and death to be the establishment of a kingdom and priesthood. In a hymn of praise Christ is honored and thanked for bestowing on his disciples such dignities.

Like the words of 1 Peter, there is a clear connection here with the Book of Exodus. The phrase "kingdom and priests" is a literal translation of the Old Testament text in which God says to the people, *"You shall be to me a priestly kingdom and a holy nation."* The promise formerly offered through Moses to the people in the desert is now an accomplished fact. Christian worshipers have been made a kingdom and priests.

When they were delivered from sin by "the blood of the Lamb" (another well-used phrase in the Book of Revelation) his followers were consecrated as priests. The saving work of the new Moses has purified his people from their sins and given them the possibility of offering true worship to God. What was promised in the old covenant by the sprinkling of an animal's blood has been realized by the shedding of Christ's blood: The sacrifice of Jesus has won spiritual deliverance for his people.

We saw a similar point being made in the Letter to the Hebrews. Because Jesus has led the way with an offering that was supremely pleasing to the Father, Christians have the liberty to enter the presence of God, freed from fear and from all other obstacles.

Just as in 1 Peter the reference to the priesthood of the faithful is best understood in a metaphorical rather than a literal sense, the evidence suggests that the same interpretation be applied to the present text of Revelation. Like the people of the Old Testament, the followers of Christ are all called priests because of their election to holiness. They are a royal priesthood in the sense of Exodus. Their vocation is to proclaim the holiness of God throughout the world. There is nothing here to identify the vocation of the whole assembly with the ministry of the altar.

"You are worthy to take the scroll and to open its seals, for you were slaughtered and by your blood you ransomed for God saints from every tribe and language and people and nation; you have made them to be a kingdom and priests serving our God, and they will reign on earth" (5:9–10). The second text of Revelation that refers to Christians as priests is set within a canticle of praise to the lordship of Christ. The writer declares that Christ has been given sovereignty over the whole world. From now on he guides the course of history. The heavenly reign of Jesus is reflected on earth by the kingly status of his followers. By the offering of the cross, Jesus has made every member of his people holy in the sight of God.

All those who believe in Christ benefit from the sacrifice he has made. Through union with him Christians offer a true sacrifice to God. Nobody washed in the blood of the Lamb is separated from the heavenly sanctuary nor excluded from intimacy with God.

The canticle does not say how exactly Christians perform their priestly duties. Given the liturgical context and the reference to the "prayers of the saints" in the preceding verse (5:8), one may conclude that the priestly functions of the followers of Christ are realized through the prayers they offer to God. Ascending like incense before the throne of God (8:3–5), the prayers of the faithful have a decisive influence on the course of human affairs.

"Blessed and holy are those who share in the first resurrection. Over these the second death has no power, but they will be priests of God and of Christ, and they will reign with him a thousand years" (20:6). This third and final reference to priests in the Book of Revelation is linked to a beatitude. Like the beatitudes in the synoptic Gospels, the purpose of the promised blessing is to encourage the followers of Christ to be faithful in moments of trial. They are assured that at some point in the future *"they will be priests."*

Spoken possibly in a time of persecution (one of the theories to explain the writing of the Book of Revelation is a background of persecution), the beatitude is intended to strengthen fidelity by giving those who are being oppressed a vision of the glory that is to come.

The disciples who are faithful will not be subject to "the second death," which is the fate of Satan and his followers (20:17). Rather they will rise to a glorious enjoyment of the presence of God as priests and kings. The martyrs who are raised to new life will have a special place before the throne of God. By their fidelity they have achieved the perfection of the Christian vocation as priests "of God and of Christ." They will be devoted to the worship of not only the Father but also of Christ: They will be fully involved in the worship of God and of the Lamb (5:14).[4]

The three texts of Revelation containing references to the priesthood of the faithful are set respectively in a hymn of praise, a canticle, and a beatitude. These texts reflect the liturgical nature of the book. They do not go beyond the metaphorical sense of priesthood derived from the Book of Exodus that we noted in 1 Peter. None of the texts uses the terms "priest" or "priesthood" in anything more than a figurative sense.

To find out the way that the Christian priesthood goes beyond a metaphorical meaning and has a ministerial sense, we have to look at another New Testament term— *presbyter*.

The Pastoral Letters

The language of church leadership employed in the New Testament has a certain fluidity. In Acts of the Apostles, 1 Peter, and the Pastoral Epistles the titles "presbyters" and "bishops" are at least partially interchangeable. But the term most generally used for those in charge of the local community is *presbyter.*

The Presbyters

The word *presbyter* means literally an "older person." People with authority called "elders" were a feature of Old Testament society. As the heads of large families or clans, they were leaders of groups. They became an official group under Moses and eased his burdens in giving judgment to the people (Num 11:16–17).

In the time of Jesus the "elders" formed part of the ruling Jewish body, the Sanhedrin. Hence, the transition to calling the appointed leaders of the Christian community "elders," as we find in Acts 14:23, was a natural one. The Acts of the Apostles describes an order of ministry in the church at Jerusalem consisting of the Twelve and a body of presbyters under them (11:30). It is entirely possible that the church in Jerusalem took from the synagogue the office of presbyter and reshaped it to fit the needs of the Christian community.

Acts informs us that on his first missionary journey, Paul appointed presbyters in the newly founded churches (14:23). Later on, in the course of his third missionary journey, Paul met the presbyters of Ephesus. He told them to feed the flock (20:17). At least by this time the two titles, "bishop" and "presbyter," seem to have indicated the same office because whereas in Acts 20:17 Paul summons the presbyters to meet him, in his speech he addresses them as bishops (20:28).

According to the evidence provided by Acts, Paul's ordinary procedure was to leave behind a body of presbyter-bishops as leaders of the communities he had founded. This at least seems to be what happened at Ephesus.

In the opening verse of his Letter to the Philippians, Paul sends greetings to the saints at Philippi, together with their "bishops" and deacons. As with the title "presbyters," the term *bishop* (overseer) was most likely taken from Judaism. There are, for example, clear parallels between the function of the Christian bishops and the presiding officials of the Qumran community.[5]

> Now as an elder myself and a witness of the sufferings of Christ, as well as one who shares in the glory to be revealed, I exhort the elders among you to tend the flock of God that is in your charge, exercising the oversight, not under compulsion but willingly, as God would have you do it—not for sordid gain but eagerly. Do not lord it over those in your charge, but be examples to the flock. And when the chief shepherd appears, you will win the crown of glory that never fades away. (1 Pet 5:1–4)

This is one of the two passages in 1 Peter that deals with public office in the church.[6] The author reminds the presbyters of their responsibilities and leaves no doubt that there was a structure of authority in the community and the leader is described as a presbyter.

1 Peter addresses the elders as a group of office bearers with a specific pastoral task. Describing Christ as the chief shepherd, the author states that the presbyters are linked to him in a special manner. The dignity of the office may also be seen in the way Peter calls himself a fellow presbyter. The warning against avarice in the exhortation also suggests that these officials had charge of the community's funds.

We have already seen that 1 Peter is a source of teaching on the priesthood of all Christians. But this work, the only book of the New Testament that mentions both priests and presbyters, never identifies the two concepts. The implication is that even though all the faithful are members of the royal priesthood, only those with a specific function of responsibility are termed presbyters. This would seem to confirm the interpretation given above that the "royal priesthood" does not refer to the ministerial priesthood. When applied to Christians as a body, the title is metaphorical. The royal priesthood designates the call of the community to lead a holy life and thereby give witness to God in the world.

The presbyters, on the other hand, are at the service of the rest of the faithful and fulfill a certain spiritual function in their behalf. The leadership of the Christian community, says 1 Peter, calls for sincere love and humility. The role of the presbyters does not set them apart from the rest of the disciples. Their function is a consequence of the priestly election of the whole church. Together all share in the mission to spread the good news.

The Pastoral Letters

The three letters of the New Testament addressed to the pastors of the church are called the "Pastoral Letters." They are the Epistles sent to Timothy and Titus, two of Paul's closest companions in his missionary work. Today most scholars believe that a later follower of Paul wrote the letters and exact dating of them is uncertain.

The distinctive feature of the Pastoral Letters, making them different from all other documents in the New Testament, is the attention they devote to ministerial offices in the community. The Pastoral Letters do not make any clear distinction between the functions of the bishop and the presbyter. The word "bishop" is always in the singular while "presbyters" is always plural. Already, then, there may have been a tendency for an individual presbyter to take the leading role among the presbyters.

According to the Pastoral Letters, the presbyters have important duties. First and foremost is their teaching role, reflecting the paramount concern of the early church to preserve intact unity of belief. The presbyters must defend the faith and protect it from false interpretation. The author urges Timothy, *"what you have heard from me through many witnesses entrust to faithful people who will be able to teach others as well"* (2 Tim 2:2).

The Pastoral Letters carefully point out the qualities necessary for those who are to be admitted to the ranks of the presbyters. Because their primary role is to be teachers of the faith, candidates must possess a sound knowledge of doctrine. Furthermore their teaching must be backed up by a good moral life. They have to be devout, just, gentle, sober, and dignified. They should be able to manage their own household well. Disqualifying factors are arrogance, greed, and drunkenness. Recent converts should not be admitted into the college of presbyters.[7]

By the time the Pastorals were composed, ordination of new ministers by the laying on of hands seems to have been the general practice: *"Do not neglect the gift that is in you, which was given to you through prophecy with the laying on of hands by the council of elders"* (1 Tim 4:14). The ceremony was a public one and the rite of laying on of hands was probably taken from the Old Testament. Joshua was appointed successor to Moses through the imposition of hands (Num 27:18–23).

Presbyters who carry out their ministry well deserve double compensation from the community. But as well as rewarding the good, Timothy is told to punish the erring and he receives an important concluding admonition: *"Do not ordain anyone hastily"* (5.22). The ordination of the wrong kind of candidates should be avoided by a careful investigation of them beforehand.

We may conclude that when the Pastorals were written the ministerial functions in the church were already established, at least in rudimentary form. Leaders were growing in authority, especially as a safeguard against false teaching. The emergence of a body of officers was taking place, even if the distinctions were still not clearly drawn. Although there are no direct references in the Pastorals to sacerdotal functions in our sense of the term, we may be sure that directing the community in so important a matter as its worship was also an integral part of the presbyters' responsibilities.

Reflections

The New Testament model of leadership is the presbyter-bishop. 1 Peter speaks of the presbyters as the leaders and ministers of the church. From the evidence of the Pauline letters and Acts, presbyters and bishops were, for all practical purposes, the same. As a group they were responsible for the pastoral care of the local churches.

From within the ranks of the presbyters there emerged, probably at varying times in different places, a leading presbyter with the rank of bishop. The evidence suggests that these leaders were appointed to take up where Paul and the other apostles left off. The presbyter-bishops were responsible for the continued care of church communities.

A number of texts list the qualities required for holding such offices. Paul or one of his disciples spells out what is expected of the presbyter-bishops as to character and work. They must be above reproach, temperate, sensible, dignified, and hospitable. In addition to having a virtuous character and being a good teacher, the one appointed to leadership must not be a recent convert nor twice married (1 Tim 3:20). We can see that the qualities required in a presbyter-bishop are more of an institutional rather than a missionary nature, indicating that when the Pastoral Letters were written a fair degree of structure had already been achieved in the community. While the presbyter is expected to be a good administrator, the New Testament also speaks of him as a pastor and a shepherd. He must at all times keep as his model the supreme pastor—the good shepherd, Jesus Christ.

The presbyter-bishops are nowhere called priests. Indeed, no Christian disciple is ever identified individually as a priest in the New Testament. The Epistle to the Hebrews only speaks of the high priesthood of Jesus by comparing his entry into heaven with the actions of the Jewish high priest who went into the Holy of Holies.

For a fuller awareness of a special Christian priesthood that took the place of the Jewish cultic ministry, a period of time had to intervene. Like many other developments in early Christianity, the understanding of the ministerial priesthood took place gradually and through the course of events.

Two developments were crucial in this regard. The first was the break with Judaism. Up to that point, the evidence suggests that Christians associated the institution of sacrificing priests with Temple worship. Acts 2:46 reports that the Jerusalem Christians went to the Temple and, as late as Acts 21:26, Paul is described as making an offering in the Temple.

The role of presiding at the Eucharist was the second factor that caused the Christian ministry to be understood as a cultic priesthood. Already in the words of institution, recorded as early as Paul's Letter to the Corinthians, some liturgical function at the eucharistic celebration is implied. The words *"Do this in remembrance of me"* were addressed to the Twelve at the Last Supper.

How precisely this officiating role was carried out is not recounted in the New Testament but the practice seems to have been taken for granted. Again we have to keep in mind that the New Testament correspondence of Paul and the other apostles tend to concentrate on problems that have arisen. They do not give full coverage of contemporary faith and practice. Only by chance do we have a reference to the Eucharist in Paul's First Letter to the Corinthians (11:17–34).

Yet we can be reasonably sure that someone did preside at the eucharistic meals and that those who participated acknowledged their right to preside. As the church grew larger, such leadership would have been regulated more precisely. In the churches addressed by Ignatius of Antioch at the beginning of the second century, only the bishop or one of the presbyters whom he designates can preside at the Eucharist (Smyrnaeans 8:1). Hence, in addition to caring for the doctrinal, moral, and even temporal needs of his flock, the bishop and his presbyters had to care for the sacramental needs of the local church as well.

But if the leaders of the community are bound in a particular way to imitate the good shepherd, all Christians are called to follow Christ. Here precisely the teaching on the royal priesthood is important for us today. There are not two classes of disciples, one within the sanctuary and the other outside. The fact that Jesus chose twelve who were to have special roles does not mean that other men and women who followed him were not also called to be disciples in the full sense of the word.

The starting point for any consideration of Christian priesthood and ministry has to be the fundamental unity of the church and the cooperation that is necessary among the people of God in their common vocation. All Christians have a part to play in the universal mission. The differences that exist in the offices of the community are the result of the special tasks assigned to each person.

One significant difference from the old dispensation is that the ministerial priests of the Christian faith are not constituted as such by birth, which was the custom in the first covenant. They are drawn from the wider community to serve the needs of the faithful. This wider community, the royal priesthood, gives them their mission. The call to come after Jesus and stay close to him is the common vocation of all.

SEVEN

The Marriage Feast of the Lamb

The Triumph of Discipleship in the Book of Revelation

In this final chapter on discipleship in the New Testament I wish to deal with an aspect of the following of Christ that is both central to the Christian faith and worrisome to many believers: The end of the world. At the turn of the millennium, as in other significant moments in history, this is a subject receiving much attention. For many people the prospect of a final consummation remains something of a horror story, a tale of fearful happenings.[1]

Before taking up the treatment of the subject in the Book of Revelation, I would like first to show that Christian concern with the end of the world has always been an important aspect of faith. This subject is addressed not only by the last book of the New Testament; the coming of the kingdom was also a concern of Paul and the first evangelists.

The earliest work of the New Testament is Paul's First Letter to the Thessalonians. Composed in the 50s, it is the first witness we have to the faith and expectations of the Christian church at the beginning. The Letter deals with the second coming, thereby revealing the preoccupation of the contemporary Christian community with the end of the world and the final Day of the Lord.

The background to this Letter is significant. According to Acts 17:5–10 Paul and his co-worker Silas had to flee from Thessalonica, a city in northern Greece, because of persecution. The opposition raised against the two apostles was probably inflicted on the young Christian community they left behind. This would have been a testing time for the new disciples and Paul responded to the situation with words of encouragement. Paul was also obliged to write to them because there had not been sufficient time to finish even the basic teaching properly. A lack of adequate instruction would explain the difficulties of the new converts and the need for clarification on certain issues.

A particular cause for concern seems to have been confusion on the matter of the second coming of Christ. The Thessalonians' belief in the nearness of this event led them to conclude that commitment to the demands of ordinary life was no longer necessary. Another misconception that Paul had to deal with was the fate of those who had died before the coming of the Lord. Paul assures his readers that the dead will not be left behind but, having been raised to new life, will in fact be the first to meet the Lord in glory:

> For the Lord himself, with a cry of command, with the archangel's call and with the sound of God's trumpet, will descend from heaven, and the dead in Christ will rise first. Then we who are alive, who are left, will be caught up in the clouds together with them to meet the Lord in the air; and so we will be with the Lord forever. Therefore encourage one another with these words. (1 Thess 4:16–18)

The first point to note here is that the teaching on the final end is given as a word of hope. In his own personal instruction to the Thessalonians, Paul, no doubt, had taught them about the death and resurrection of Christ. These events mark the beginning of the end-time. Even if they must endure persecution, Paul urges the members of the community to hold on to the expectation of a glorious and imminent coming of Christ.

While they grieve for their dead, Christians are not to be like those who have no hope (4:13). They are consoled by the belief that once the Lord returns they will all experience the power of the resurrection. Those who have "fallen asleep in Christ" will be raised and together with the living they shall be taken up to meet the Lord in the air.

Paul probably believed that the second coming would be within his own lifetime. This is why he reacted so confidently in the face of opposition. Christ's return from heaven would be seen by all, persecuted and persecutors alike. As they underwent affliction, the expectation of an imminent coming would have given Paul and his converts the courage they needed to hang on in the face of trials.

Yet, though Paul believed the second coming to be close, he gave no precise hour or date. His understanding was that it would come suddenly and unexpectedly. So the followers of Christ should stay wide awake and be sober. Vigilance is a theme that surfaces in the Letter to the Thessalonians in a number of places.

Paul does not attempt to frighten his readers with graphic accounts of the last days. No details of the event are given. Paul's chief concern is to calm the anxieties of the community he had so recently brought to the faith. Both the living and the dead will be joyfully united to the Lord at his second coming.

The coming kingdom of God is also central to the first Gospel. Mark portrays Jesus as a prophet who came to usher in the last times: *"Jesus came to Galilee, proclaiming the good news of God, and saying, 'The time is fulfilled, and the kingdom of God has come near; repent, and believe in the good news'"* (1:14–15).

Jesus not only preached about this event, but he gathered twelve disciples who were chosen to be the signs of the renewal of Israel in the last times. Through his miracles and, in particular, by delivering people from demonic possession, Jesus showed that the power of evil in the world was being broken.

There was an even more arresting way Jesus linked himself to the expectation of the final coming that was current in his day: He accepted baptism at the hands of John.

In submitting himself to the water rite of John at the beginning of his ministry, Jesus pronounced himself a disciple of the fiery prophet of the Last Judgment.[2]

Jesus approved of John and regarded him as an authentic prophet. *"Truly I tell you, among those born of women no one has arisen greater than John the Baptist"* (Mt 11:11). He praised John for his uncompromising stand against wickedness and his proclamation of imminent judgment on all Israel. Even though he himself proclaimed the coming of God as a moment of salvation rather than of punishment, Jesus basically affirmed John's message.

During his public ministry, Jesus' preaching of the coming kingdom of God pervaded every aspect of his life, his miracles, and his teaching. Throughout the gospel tradition one point is constantly repeated: "Jesus did understand the central symbol of the kingdom of God in terms of the definitive coming of God in the near future to bring the present state of things to an end and to establish his full and unimpeded rule over the world in general and Israel in particular."[3]

Yet Jesus plainly admitted that he did not know the divine timetable for the end of the world. Rather he instructed his disciples to pray fervently for the coming of God's kingdom. We find this insistence in the prayer he taught as his own: the Lord's Prayer.

The banquets at which Jesus participated with the outcasts of society were a clear expression of the joyful nature of the coming kingdom of God. The hungry would be satisfied and those in mourning would rejoice. As promised in the beatitudes, the poor would finally inherit the land and enjoy the vision of God. The coming kingdom would mean the reversal of the unjust structures of the present world and bring the reward of those who had proved faithful in their trials. In the presence of Jesus the poor could rejoice in the sure promise that they would experience a reversal of their fortunes. Sinners flocked to his company and ate with him.

A wit has said that the task of a prophet is to comfort the afflicted and to afflict the comfortable. If John the Baptist's warnings of doom fit into the category of a prophet who afflicts the comfortable, Jesus' preaching on the coming reign of God was one of comfort for the afflicted. Though preaching about the coming of the kingdom, Jesus was not indifferent to the realities of the present world. His disciples were told to live with confidence in the providence of their heavenly Father and to pray to him as the One who would give them what they needed to eat and drink.

Jesus not only predicted the future coming of the kingdom; he also taught that it was present through his life and teaching. *"The kingdom of God is among you,"* he told the Pharisees who wanted to know when the kingdom would come (Lk 17:21). Jesus refused to give exact details about future events; instead he directed his listeners to examine their own experience for signs of God's activity.

The presence of Jesus meant that God's reign was breaking in upon the world. He pointed to his miracles as proof that the time of healing had finally arrived. Among these signs, deliverance of people from the power of demons had a special place. Exorcisms are in fact the most common form of miracle found in the synoptic Gospels. They are revealing pointers to the role of Jesus as the prophet of the end-time. *"But if it is by the finger of God that I cast out the demons, then the kingdom of God has come to you"* (Lk 11:20).

While announcing the imminent coming of God's kingly rule, Jesus showed in his own person that Satan's hold on the world had been broken. Mastery over the forces of darkness complemented the preaching of Jesus. The power of evil could not withstand him. The dominance of Jesus over the demonic world was intended to inspire his disciples with confidence during their moments of trial. The same message suffuses the Book of Revelation.

The Book of Revelation

The last work of the New Testament, the Book of Revelation, is both puzzling and popular with readers. Speaking of the end of the world and using such symbols as the Scarlet Woman and the Beast whose number is 666, Revelation contains some of the best known images in the whole of Scripture. Like the rest of the Bible, the book contains a divine message. This is in fact the meaning of the original Greek title, the *Apocalypse* (Revelation). What gives the book its unique flavor is the colorful way in which the revelation is communicated:

> The revelation of Jesus Christ, which God gave him to show his servants what must soon take place; he made it known by sending his angel to his servant John, who testified to the word of God and to the testimony of Jesus Christ, even to all that he saw. Blessed is the one who reads aloud the words of the prophecy, and blessed are those who hear and who keep what is written in it; for the time is near. (Rev 1:1–3)

The Book of Revelation is a prophecy. The author makes this clear in his introduction. Obviously a Christian, he narrates the revelation God gave him in the prophetic forms of the Old Testament. Our understanding of the Book of Revelation changes when we see it as part of a tradition of Jewish Scripture rather than a highly individualistic piece of writing. Speaking usually to deal with situations of contemporary crisis, the prophets gave a religious interpretation of the events of history. They tended to be more interested in the direction of events, where they were going, rather than their origins. They reminded their hearers of eternal values.

There was a strong element of judgment in the later prophetical writings of the Old Testament and this aspect eventually took precedence over everything else. The authors of this literature were concerned to preserve the faith of their communities. They did not delve into mysteries for their own sake. They wrote for the benefit and support of their people, not to dazzle, bewilder, or frighten them.

The prophets believed that the real significance of human history would only be fully revealed when we stand before the final judgment of God. They understood history to have a predetermined course and duration. At the same time this faith did not undermine their acceptance of human freedom. On the contrary, they appealed to their listeners to change their ways and live according to the commandments of God.

Such features also abound in the Book of Revelation. As we saw already, there was a belief among the early Christians that the world was in its final stages. The death and resurrection of Jesus had ushered in the last days. The author of Revelation responds to this expectation in the style of prophetical literature. He puts over his message through the use of visions, oracles, symbolic actions, threats, hymns, speeches, laments, and warnings.

We find similar imagery in the Book of Ezekiel. His visions provide many of the figures of speech that are used in the Book of Revelation. Other prophets also made use of this kind of language. Zechariah has visions of lamp stands, scrolls, and four differently colored horses.

The prophetic works of the Old Testament were couched in vivid language to convince wavering hearts about what would happen at the end of history. This style of writing became prominent after the Babylonian Exile (c. 609–538 B.C.). The shattering realization of their powerlessness made the people realize that an earthly salvation based on human effort was becoming more and more unlikely. The later persecution of the Jews by the Greek kings brought this process to a climax. The most popular work of this era was the Book of Daniel.

Like the Book of Daniel, Revelation had a public message and was not intended solely for private circulation. Far from having a secret teaching for a privileged few, the author was conscious of giving a communication that concerned the future of the whole church. He did not withdraw into some private domain to derive personal consolation from the divine message. He was conscious of a responsibility to make the revelation known to his contemporaries so that they too could be strengthened by the knowledge of God's coming judgment on the world.

Even though the references to Jesus Christ constitute the major difference between Revelation and other Jewish works of the same genre, the difference in the tone of the writing is not as extensive as we might expect. The primary task of both Jewish and Christian prophets was the encouragement of the faithful.

Even in the details of the writing, Christ's mission as portrayed in Revelation conforms to what can be read in the traditional Jewish literature about the heavenly warrior and his adherents. In both cases the faithful are those who remain steadfastly loyal to their leader, despite persecution. Like the heroes of the Old Testament, Jesus inspires his disciples to follow him and make sacrifices in the hope of eternal salvation.

There are many elements in the Book of Revelation that align it with other literature of the prophetic type. But of course there are differences as well. First of all, unlike most of the Old Testament prophets, the author of Revelation does not present his work as an oracle spoken directly in the name of the Lord. His visions come indirectly through the mediation of an angel (1:1).

The Book of Revelation has some remarkably distinctive imagery. Jesus Christ is not only the supreme warrior and the great judge of the world; he is also the Lamb of God and the One who has overcome the powers of evil by his death on the cross. His followers can wash their robes clean in the blood of this Lamb.

The Lamb is the dominant figure of the Book of Revelation. This is the crucial difference from other Jewish writing. The subject of the narrative is the person of Jesus and, in particular, his victory on the cross. Christ's triumph over death is a foretaste of the final victory over the powers of evil at the end of the world. The assurance of the ultimate salvation brought by the Lamb who was slain and has been raised by God is the overriding message of the prophet who composed the Book of Revelation.

The Book of Revelation is not, then, in the final analysis, about the end of the world; rather, it's about the closeness of Jesus to the present moment. The reader is not given a threatening glimpse of the last judgment, but a reassuring message that God is the power that rules the universe. Christ is present in the midst of each faithful community. He is the one who truly decides the course of history.

The story narrated in the Book of Revelation is not a detailed preview of the final conflict between the forces of evil and the Lord of History but a word of comfort about the direction of human affairs. The Lamb of God leads his disciples in their struggle with the demonic powers and the false prophets. The tension between their faith and their experience of evil in the world threatens to undermine the belief of many Christians. If Christ holds the ultimate power over the world, why do his followers have to endure so much? The Book of Revelation is a response to this fundamental question.

Consequently, though the message of Revelation is anchored in the experience of the author, it cannot be limited to his time. Coded in symbolic language, the prophet's words speak to later generations also. Certain images may indeed refer to such contemporary figures as the Roman emperor, but they point to a reality that is experienced not only in Roman times but also in other periods of history.

According to tradition, the Book of Revelation was written for the encouragement of the Christian community during the persecution of the emperor Domitian (c. A.D. 90). Revelation does mention the author's banishment (1:9) and the expectation of disciples being arrested (2:10). The prophet's visions convey the probability of intense persecution in the near future. Yet whether the purpose of the book can be located in such a precise historical setting has recently been disputed.

Without positing a setting of actual persecution, one could also interpret the book as a clash between Christian belief and the actual life situation in which faith is lived out. In this way, Revelation can indeed be interpreted as an answer to a crisis, but one that is always present for the Christian faithful. The struggle results from the inherent strain between the followers of Christ and the social reality within which they live. Christians have to endure a continuing pattern of persecution and rejection.

In his introduction, the author states that he is addressing his prophecy in the form of a public pastoral letter to *"the seven churches that are in Asia"* (1:4). The seven messages to the churches are then cast in the form of individual letters.

After the opening three chapters, the book centers on a series of great visions. Again the number seven dominates: There are seven seals, seven trumpets, seven secrets, and seven bowls. The book ends by coming back to the literary form of a letter and concludes with a benediction.[4]

The author does not divide his text into completely separate sections but links them together. This interweaving can create confusion in the mind of the reader who is looking for clear divisions in the text. The forward thrust of the work is also interrupted by interludes in the form of hymns and acclamations. These function in a manner similar to a Greek chorus commenting on the actions of the principal actors of the drama. The action is maintained through the repetition of images and visions flowing from each other and intermixing as they build up towards the final triumph.

The well-known symbols that the author adapts from the Old Testament are sometimes used in contrasting pairs. The key image of the Lamb is placed in confrontation with the Beast; the great harlot is a contrast to the woman of chapter 12; and the New Jerusalem replaces Babylon.

"I was in the spirit on the Lord's day, and I heard behind me a loud voice like a trumpet saying, 'Write in a book what you see and send it to the seven churches, to Ephesus, to Smyrna, to Pergamum, to Thyatira, to Sardis, to Philadelphia, and to Laodicea'" (1:10–11). The seven letters of the first three chapters give us the main clue to understanding the whole book. They enable us to see from the beginning that the work of the writer is directed to a practical purpose.

Although the prophet's revelation goes beyond the local situation of the seven churches and has a permanent value, he starts with these particular circumstances and gives us concrete details about them. The book is not therefore a wild dream divorced from historical fact, but a poetical attempt to deal with certain concrete issues in light of the author's belief in what is to come. The seven letters have a number of similarities but also differ significantly among themselves. Only the churches of Smyrna and Philadelphia escape censure completely while nothing positive is said about the churches of Sardis and Laodicea.

Three types of problems confront the seven churches: false teaching, persecution, and complacency. The prophet is not only concerned to encourage the disciples under persecution; he is equally strong in the insistence on sound teaching. The severest judgment is directed to the spiritual tepidity of the seventh church, Laodicea, *"because you are lukewarm, and neither cold nor hot, I am about to spit you out of my mouth"* (3:16).

Even though they are referred to as "letters," these communications were most likely not sent to the individual churches in the ordinary way. They do not, for example, follow the form of Paul's Letters to the churches he founded. Rather they are prophetic messages. They all start with a standard prophetic formula: *"These are the words of the first and the last, who was dead and came to life"* (2:8). Each communication ends with a call for attentiveness: *"Let anyone who has an ear listen to what the Spirit is saying to the churches"* (3:22).

The promises of future happiness scattered throughout the letters anticipate the description of glory found in the concluding chapters of Revelation. Again they remind us that the purpose of the prophet is not to intimidate his readers with alarming visions, but to encourage them with the promise of what lies in store for those who are faithful.

The call to fidelity is the basic theme of all seven letters and, in this regard, they encapsulate the message of the rest of the book. Those who endure to the end in each of the churches are promised an unfailing reward for their labors.

The Lamb and the Dragon

The Chinese proverb that "one picture is worth a thousand words" would have been wholeheartedly endorsed by the author of Revelation. As a Christian visionary, he replaces the narrative style of the Old Testament prophets with a visual form that is ultimately his own original creation. The vitality and profusion of his visions, their interweaving and interlocking nature, and the dramatic power of the story all contribute to make him the greatest artist of the New Testament.

To get his message across and make his point as effectively as possible the writer employs vivid, colorful language. Typical of many ancient tales, the animal figures speak and act. The universe of the prophet is divided into heaven, earth, and the underworld, the abode of the demons. He speaks of great portents in heaven, sacred scrolls, and seven stars. He is caught up in mystery but, despite the interpretations of some later commentators, he is not interested in mystification. Concealed messages or unfathomable meanings are not his concern.

The variety and exuberance of the imagery help us to see how the author conveyed his message. He did not, like the prophets of old, just *speak* of heavenly realities. He *sees* them. So, for example, he transforms his message on the sins of the people into a vision of the scarlet woman. In this way the visions convey his message in pictures. Revelation tells the reader what John "saw." All the material of the prophets—hymns, speeches, and personal reflections—are placed within the visions. The visual takes precedence over all other forms of reporting.

Like the seven letters that introduce the narrative of Revelation, John's visions are directed to deepening the faith of the Christian communities. "John's visions were directed by a desire, not to mystify either the Christians or the imperial authorities, but to *promote spiritual insight.* They were to manifest that 'most important characteristic of symbols, namely their power to direct our thinking and our orientation towards life.'"[5]

> Then I saw between the throne and the four living creatures and among the elders a Lamb standing as if it had been slaughtered, having seven horns and seven eyes, which are the seven spirits of God sent out into all the earth. He went and took the scroll from the right hand of the one who was seated on the throne. When he had taken the scroll, the four living creatures and the twenty-four elders fell before the Lamb, each holding a harp and golden bowls full of incense, which are the prayers of the saints. They sing a new song: "You are worthy to take the scroll and to open its seals, for you were slaughtered and by your blood you ransomed for God saints from every tribe and language and people and nation . . . ." (5:6–9)

This vision of the heavenly court and the Lamb sets the scene for everything that is to follow. The introductory seven letters have described the situation of the Christian communities in Asia from the point of view of their earthly condition. Now John directs our attention to the divine majesty who holds the ultimate power over the fate of these churches. Because Jesus Christ has been victorious over the forces of evil, he shares the glory of God in heaven. He is the Lamb who exercises true lordship over the world. The images employed in this opening vision will occur again and again throughout the book. They are here solemnly introduced.

The focus of the picture is the figure of the Lamb, the victor who has been put to death but has risen again. Introduced here for the first time, the "slain but standing Lamb" is the dominant title for Christ in the Book of Revelation, occurring twenty-eight times.

A Lamb *"standing as if it had been slaughtered"* is clearly a reference to the death on Calvary. The description of the

Lamb who has been sacrificed would have been familiar to Christian readers and is possibly based on what the fourth Gospel says about the Lamb of God. John's Gospel and the Book of Revelation are the only places in the New Testament where "the Lamb" is used as a designation for Christ. John the Baptist in reference to Jesus uses the title on two occasions (Jn 1:29, 36).

The emphasis on the "slain but standing Lamb" brings to mind both the death of Jesus and his resurrection. There is also an indirect reference to the Old Testament, through the Passover lamb whose blood saved the Jews from the destroying angel. The slaughter of the paschal lamb was an image quickly adopted by the early church to interpret the death of Jesus (1 Cor 5:7). The image evokes the deliverance of the Jews from slavery. The victory of the Lamb is a new Exodus for his people.

The power of the Lamb is emphasized by his appearance. The seven horns and the seven eyes, which are the seven spirits of God sent out into the earth (5:6), signify fullness of power and control of the destiny of the world. Because of his might, the Lamb is the only one in the whole universe who is able to open the scroll.

The seven-sealed scroll has been interpreted in different ways. Some ancient ceremonies for the enthronement of a king included the acceptance of a book in which the destiny of the world was inscribed. Securing this book meant that the ruler was given responsibility for the execution of justice. Acquainted with such a tradition or not, the prophet sees the enthronement of the Lamb as constituting him judge of the world and ruler of its destiny.

Although the breaking of the seven seals and the opening of the scroll unleash upon the earth the calamities of the final days, the prophet does not say that these disasters are directly caused by the Lamb. Though they do not happen without the permission of God, they are the direct result of the unholy structures that govern the world's affairs. In a similar perspective, the four horsemen are symbols of the contemporary miseries brought about by the abuses of Roman rule: war, plague, famine, and death.[6]

Opposed to the Lamb is the Dragon. He and his minions first opposed Michael and the angels in heaven: *"Michael and his angels fought against the dragon. The dragon and his angels fought back, but they were defeated, and there was no longer any place for them in heaven. The great dragon was thrown down, that ancient serpent, who is called the Devil and Satan, the deceiver of the whole world—he was thrown down to the earth, and his angels were thrown down with him"* (12: 7–9).

The victory of the Lamb is at the same time the defeat of the Dragon. Both can be located in the death and resurrection of Jesus Christ. The conflict between the Lamb and the Dragon continues on earth through the witness and martyrdom of the followers of Jesus. The struggle between the forces of good and evil are pictured in the visions of conflict that follow in the Book of Revelation.[7]

As we read these accounts and reflect on their significance we have to keep in mind that Revelation is trying to express the inexpressible. The visions have to be taken collectively if we are to allow them to speak to us. We have to keep firmly in mind that the particular details of each vision are of secondary significance. What is important is the basic pattern of persecution followed by divine judgment and final salvation for the faithful followers of the Lamb that is the core meaning of each symbolic account.

The visions of Revelation look at what has been going on since the beginning of recorded history until the present. They mark the different epochs as a struggle for justice that will not have its final outcome until the second coming of Jesus who is *"the Alpha and the Omega, the first and the last, the beginning and the end"* (22:13).

Allied to the Dragon are the two beasts that come from the sea and the land (13:1–18). These creatures recall the sea monster and the land monster of the Old Testament. They are often taken to represent the destructive might of Rome and the imperial cult.

Also ranged on the side of the Dragon are the prostitute and the power of Babylon. These may have been symbols of the corrupt civilization of the time. They are the enemies who will fall before the all-conquering blood of the Lamb.

But before the final defeat they have the capacity to wreak havoc on the earth, even among the disciples of Christ.

The task of the Lamb is not merely to execute judgment on the world but, above all, to deliver the faithful Christians from the power of evil. As the visions roll on, the salvation theme takes on more force. Like the fourth Gospel, the Book of Revelation uses different symbols of life with cumulative effect. Besides the tree of life, the crown of life, and the book of life mentioned in the opening chapters, Revelation gives a graphic account of the energizing properties of the water of life in its concluding section.

The symbol of light is also to be found. The last two chapters describe the illumination the presence of the Lamb gives to the New Jerusalem (21:23) and the divine light that is shed on his servants (22:5).

Another point of contact with the Gospel of John is the way Revelation speaks of salvation as a present and not merely a future reality. Already now the Christian can draw life and light from the presence in the church of the resurrected Christ. He is the Lamb who was slain but now stands triumphantly in the midst of his disciples:

> Then I looked, and there was the Lamb, standing on Mount Zion! And with him were one hundred forty-four thousand who had his name and his Father's name written on their foreheads. And I heard a voice from heaven like the sound of many waters and like the sound of loud thunder; the voice I heard was like the sound of harpists playing on their harps, and they sing a new song before the throne and before the four living creatures and before the elders. (14:1–3)

The vision of the Lamb on Mount Zion surrounded by a host of followers reinforces the belief that Christ leads his people in their confrontation with the Dragon and his hirelings. Jesus is alive and well, though his presence is only known to those with faith. The Christian interpretation of history views the resurrection of Jesus as the event that not only points to the future glory of the human race but also implies that the Lord is present among his people in their earthly struggles.

Mount Zion is the counter-image of the sea from which the Beast emerges. The one hundred and forty-four thousand are those who were sealed from the twelve tribes (7:1–8). The seal is the name of the Lamb and the name of the Father on their foreheads. This distinguishes them from the followers of the Beast who are also marked on their foreheads (13:16). This special group of the elect have given their lives for Christ. Those who have been put to death for their faith are identified in a special way with the Lamb who was slain.

The association of the one hundred and forty-four thousand with the Lamb is the anticipation of final victory. Because they have followed the Lamb when he ascended Mount Zion to make his great sacrifice, they also accompany him when he enters the New Jerusalem. The climax of the Book of Revelation is not the overthrow of the Dragon and his cohorts, but the great marriage supper of the Lamb with his Bride in the City of Light.

The Lamb and the Bride

"'Let us rejoice and exult and give him the glory, for the marriage of the lamb has come, and his bride has made herself ready; to her it has been granted to be clothed with fine linen, bright and pure'—for the fine linen is the righteous deeds of the saints" (19:7-8). The last three chapters of the Book of Revelation form a triumphant conclusion to the prophet's visions. A glorious wedding ceremony is the image he employs to describe the blissful resolution of the conflicts that have racked his story.[8]

The author of Revelation uses nuptial symbolism as the best means at his disposal to depict the final outcome of God's grand plan of salvation. The marriage of the Lamb with his Bride poetically describes the reward of the saints who have proved faithful to the end. The New Jerusalem is the scene where this great act of communion takes place.

Here again we see the influence of the Old Testament prophets. A comparison of the relationship of God with his people to a marriage is a simile found in their writings. Hosea in particular was keen on this imagery. He depicted idolatry as a breaking of the marriage bond with Yahweh.

Yet in the Book of Revelation the term *Bridegroom* is never directly applied to Jesus. He is referred to as "the Lamb" (5:6). The standing Lamb is the symbol of the risen Christ. In this sense he is presented from the beginning as ready for the final celebration. His triumph over death has made the marriage possible. What remains to be accomplished is the final victory of all the saints over death and sin.

These symbols point, of course, to a mystery that cannot be fully explained or grasped. "Both the realistic terminology and the nuptial imagery fail to adequately describe the realities to which they point. The wedding image bears within it the meaning of self-donation and union through love. This is particularly apt to describe the relationship between the Risen Christ and the Church."[9]

The Lamb is no ordinary Bridegroom. Through his sacrificial death Christ has brought into existence the church that is called to be his Bride. His love holds the church together and his cleansing action purifies her of evil works. As the future Bride of the Lamb, the earthly church is presented in chapters 1 to 3 as still struggling to find her way and to prepare for the forthcoming marriage. The resurrected One calls the seven churches to correct their faults and emend their ways before his final appearance.

The purpose of these prophetical messages is to bring the different communities up to the level of love required by their vocation to be the Bride of the Lamb. The disciples in each of the seven churches have to examine themselves and renew their efforts to live in love, faith, service, and endurance.

Though in a state of betrothal to the Lamb, the churches are guilty of infidelity when they forget their wonderful destiny. Even worse than outright rejection of the proposed marriage is indifference to the expectant Bridegroom. The lukewarm response of Laodicea (3:15–18) is the most galling of all. Only when their love is fully mature will he bring them to the banquet of the heavenly wedding.

The victory of the Lamb is assured. From the start he is depicted as standing before the throne of God. The final victory of the Bride over the forces of evil is not so depicted. Her fate is the theme of the conflict between good and evil worked out in the course of history. Only those who emerge victorious from the struggle are found worthy to take their place at the wedding banquet of the Lamb.

The love of the Lamb will bond his followers from all peoples and tongues into one harmonious community in the New Jerusalem. This happy conclusion will be the fulfillment of the promise given by Jesus to the seven churches: *"I am coming soon; hold fast to what you have, so that no one may seize your crown. If you conquer, I will make you a pillar in the temple of my God; you will never go out of it. I will write on you the name of my God, and the name of the city of my God, the new Jerusalem that comes down from my God out of heaven, and my own new name"* (3:11–12).

The Book of Revelation presents the New Jerusalem as the eternal abode of the saints. In the present world they are being prepared like a bride for her husband. For the Lamb the task has been accomplished; for the seven churches, the future Bride of the Lamb, the struggle continues. When they are freed from the evil works of Babylon, the city of the damned, the citizens of New Jerusalem will be adorned with fine linen, bright and clean.

"Then I saw a new heaven and new earth; for the first heaven and the first earth had passed away, and the sea was no more. And I saw the holy city, the new Jerusalem, coming down out of heaven from God, prepared as a bride adorned for her husband" (21:1–2). The last two chapters of Revelation are given over to a magnificent portrait of the final glory of the elect. The rampaging Dragon has been totally defeated and cast into the lake of fire where he has disappeared, never to re-emerge. Now the author gives all his attention to the marriage between the Lamb and his city-Bride.

The Lamb sustains the communion of love. He is the one who gives light to the city: *"And the city has no need of sun or moon to shine on it, for the glory of God is its light, and its lamp is the Lamb"* (21:23). Through the Bridegroom the light of glory illuminates the New Jerusalem. The crystal clearness of the city is a reflection of the Lamb's pure and intense love.

The city is big enough to hold all the saints of history but within its walls only the holy are present. The Lamb has fashioned for himself a Bride who is worthy to take her place in the New Jerusalem because of her fidelity in time of trial. God's elect together with the Bridegroom form the sacred place so there is no need for a temple.

The Book of Revelation concludes with a glowing description of the fruitfulness of the marriage between the Lamb and his Bride. Their union is dynamic and productive. To convey an idea of this fruitfulness the prophet picks up more symbols from the Old Testament: The river of life and the tree of life:

> Then the angel showed me the river of the water of life, bright as crystal, flowing from the throne of God and of the Lamb through the middle of the street of the city. On either side of the river is the tree of life with its twelve kinds of fruit, producing its fruit each month; and the leaves of the tree are for the healing of the nations. (22:1–2)

The life-giving waters that flow from the throne of the Lamb mirror Ezekiel's vision of the water flowing from the Temple (47:1–12). There are also allusions to the Garden of Eden. The love of the Lamb produces fruits that even outstrip what was created in the first earthly paradise.

Thus the Book of Revelation ends by bringing us full circle: The conclusion takes us back to the first chapters of the Bible. Like a great rainbow, the treasures of God are found at both ends. But whereas the first paradise was fragile and easily destroyed by the machinations of the evil one, there is no possibility of a recurrence of the early loss for the followers of the Lamb. They rest secure in his love. He is the lamp of the city of God and from him there flows a source of unfailing energy to satisfy all the desires of his elected Bride.

The Bible ends by taking us back to the vision of the Creation. It ties together our origins and our destiny. Where we have come from and where we are going are linked together in the marvelous design of God.

Reflections

The Book of Revelation narrates the victory of the standing Lamb over evil. This triumph gives hope to the disciples of Jesus. The composer judges all human activities from the viewpoint of the ultimate triumph of the divine power. His outlook is beyond the historical in the sense that he rises above the boundaries of time. Like a musical conductor looking at his score, he sees what has been played, what is being played, and what will be played.[10]

In the prophet's visions there is no strict division between the present age and the age that is to come. There is fluidity between the different time zones. From his lofty perspective he sees the new heaven and the new earth suddenly swimming into view. Jesus Christ is the decisive factor of the coming transformation. His death and resurrection are the signs that the power of God will eventually destroy the grip of evil on the world.

The intermeshing time zones of Revelation mean that the book can be read with three periods in mind: the past, the present, and the future. Each of the time frames has a particular bearing on Christian discipleship.

Despite what may appear to the contrary, the present activity of Christ, in the time of the church and on behalf of the church, is the prophet's foremost concern. This can be seen as his opening statement of intent in the letters to the seven churches. The Christian is called to be steadfast and do battle with the powers of evil. The visions of the prophet function as an encouragement to fidelity in the here and now.

The contemporary ring of Revelation is also brought out by the fact that in addition to the visions of what is to come, much present activity is also narrated. Indeed there are more than twice as many references to present activity as there are to past action (49 to 19). Also, despite the strong future orientation of the book, there are more references to present activity than to future actions (49 to 41). The author comes back again and again to the present.[11]

The blood of the Lamb that was shed is still effective for the world today. Christ is present in the churches, which he loves, rebukes, disciplines, gives time to repent, and bestows grace upon. He continues to speak through his Christian prophets. The following of Christ is not therefore a passive interlude between the first and the second coming, but a vital response in one's present life situation. We who read the Book of Revelation are also part of the narrative. "The Christian's story corresponds to the Christ's story: as conquering/dying was the key event in Jesus' life, so it is the meaning of discipleship in the present."[12]

EIGHT

Following Christ on the Way

We have looked at the teaching of the New Testament on discipleship under seven different headings. These provide us with seven different models of discipleship, each one offering a unique view of the subject. Like the seven pillars of wisdom, our sources have given us insights from complementary angles.

Our starting point was religious experience. We are very much aware today of the role that religious experience plays in the spiritual journey. Few would deny that the beginning of all religious commitment is some kind of personal encounter with God. This may come in different ways: Through the incidents of life or through people we meet. No doubt all of us can look back and find some event that was important for our religious development.

Personal experience was central to the vocation of the first disciples. Jesus called them directly. But Paul provides us with a more accessible model as we reflect on our lives. Like us, he was not one of "the Twelve." He had no contact with the earthly Jesus. Furthermore he speaks at length of his experience and describes the effects of his conversion to Christ.

For Paul the founding event of his life as a follower of Christ took place on the road to Damascus. He describes this moment as the basis of his later life. Yet there is a certain lack of clarity in his reports of the event. Even for Paul it remained something of a mystery, though he was convinced the Lord had touched him.

Paul's encounter influenced his life and opinions in a very definite way. He had the experience and grasped its meaning. Through his single vision of Jesus in glory something became immediately clear to him. The Jesus whom he had considered a betrayer was suddenly revealed in glory as the risen Lord. This vision overturned his previous convictions. His prejudices were shattered in an instant.

If experience was the constant reference point of Paul's life, the meeting on the road to Damascus did not take place in a vacuum. Paul needed to integrate himself into the Christian community. This was in existence before he came on the scene and was already branching out in a worldwide mission. Paul learned from his fellow believers and had to submit his preaching to their scrutiny.

Another significant factor of Paul's conversion was his cultural background. Not merely a Jew, but a Jew of the Roman world, Paul was sophisticated enough to interpret his vision and its signification on a far wider scale: As the risen Christ, Jesus was the Lord of history. He was not solely for the Jewish people; his message was much broader and even universal.

Paul's response to the message of Jesus is summed up in his vision of Christianity as lived "in Christ." The phrase captured succinctly the meaning of his faith. In this he laid down a path for all future followers of Jesus. Our lives too are built upon our personal experience of Jesus; they are meant to be lived "in Christ."

Paul remained immersed in the society of his day. His conversion did not push him into monastic seclusion. He traveled incessantly, seeking out new places to evangelize. He took on the greatest intellectual challenge of his day, the Greek world, and founded churches within its borders. The communities he started on the Greek mainland were to remain the most enduring legacy of his missionary work.

Our second consideration of discipleship in the New Testament passed from the call of the disciple to the implications of the call. Mark's Gospel is a narrative of the way of discipleship. The followers of Jesus have to walk behind the master on the way to Calvary in order to reach the glory of the resurrection. Jesus has first traveled this road and so must every Christian.

Matthew focuses on the presence of Christ in the church, a presence that will be with us to the end of time. Because he is present, Jesus can invite his followers to take up the yoke of his law. This yoke is not to be oppressive because Jesus gives rest to those who feel heavily burdened. The revelation that Jesus himself has received from the Father is passed on to his followers and strengthens them in their difficulties.

The first historian of the church, Luke, points out the continuity of God's action through the life of Jesus and the work of the first apostles. The source of this unity is the gift of the Holy Spirit. Luke also stresses the need for poverty among the disciples. He calls to mind the attitude of the early Christians who shared everything in common. He connects the year of Jubilee with the beginning of Jesus' preaching. The year of the Lord's favor is a time for the pardoning of debts and reconciliation.

Women as disciples have an important part to play in Luke/Acts. The evangelist sees them as the most faithful followers of Jesus. In a special way Luke portrays the Spirit active in Mary. She conceives her Son by the power of the Spirit. She prays with the disciples in preparation for Pentecost. She is the perfect disciple.

Life in the Spirit is depicted by John's Gospel as a union of the vine and the branches. Jesus is the life of the world and he bestows the life of grace on his disciples through the sacraments, especially the Eucharist. The divine nature of Jesus, his pre-existence, and his divine power are highlighted in John more than in any other work of the New Testament. All other themes are telescoped into this one grand vision.

The response of the members of John's community to the revelation of the Word has to be faith. Such faith is not merely intellectual acceptance of the teaching of Jesus, but rather a wholehearted allegiance to him.

The Letter to the Hebrews was written to give the followers of Jesus assurance in their commitment. Through his offering on the cross Jesus has become their great high priest. Though during his lifetime he was not reckoned a priest, his sacrifice on Calvary has constituted him the supreme intercessor for his people. In their struggles they know that they have a mediator in heaven who is continually interceding for them before the throne of God. The prayer of the high priest gives them the boldness to enter the heavenly sanctuary.

The Book of Revelation speaks about the last things and the advent of the kingdom of God. Revelation is a call to repentance and a promise of the triumph of Christ over the power of Satan. It paints a vivid picture of the relentless struggle between the forces of good and evil in the world. The combat will continue until the final victory of the Lamb and his followers.

Revelation concludes with a magnificent description of the final consummation. This is depicted as a marriage banquet in which the Lamb is finally united with his Bride, the church. The New Jerusalem, the city of peace and joy, will be the eternal abode of Christ and those who have been faithful to the Lamb.

We have looked at the various traditions found in the New Testament and identified the particular characteristics of each one. However, as Gregory the Great once remarked, we have heard the facts, now we have to enter into the mystery. Like the other early Church Fathers, Gregory considered the literal sense of Scripture as only the first step of the ladder. Other, more important steps had to be climbed if the Word of God was to achieve its purpose. These steps were, above all, the spiritual and moral applications of the text. For this reason, "climbing the steps of understanding" was not merely a human enterprise for the early commentators, but was, above all, a gift of the divine Spirit.

To change the metaphor to another favorite of theirs, the Fathers believed that the boat of human understanding could only cross the sea of sacred Scripture if the Holy Spirit gave wind to the sail. The Spirit has to be present as the inspiration of the original author and in the hearts of those who open themselves to his presence as they endeavor to understand the text.

With this image in mind I would like to conclude by quoting another part of the prayer of St. Hilary, cited in the Preface. He asks God to complement his labors with the grace of the Holy Spirit and thereby bring his efforts to their desired end:

> I must also pray for the gift of your help and your mercy, that you may fill the sails which we have spread of our belief and confession of faith with the breath of your Spirit, and so drive us along the course of preaching you which I have begun. For he who said: "Ask and it will be given you; seek and you will find; knock, and it will be opened to you," will not be unfaithful to his promise. (*De Trinitate* 7–8)

 Notes

Preface

1. H. Anderson, *The Gospel of Mark*, London 1981, 21.

2. Quoted in R. C. Collins, *Introduction to the New Testament*, London 1992, 380.

3. The attempt to reconstruct, at least in basic outline, the life of Jesus of Nazareth continues to exercise an attraction. The most ambitious effort in our own day is the research of the American J. Meier, though he admits the limitations of the project he has undertaken. He underlines the difficulty of classifying Jesus in the context of his own time with the very title of his work: *A Marginal Jew,* 2 Vols., New York 1991–94.

4. Cf. *De Trinitate* 1:37–38.

Chapter One

1. J. Fitzmyer, *According to Paul*, New York 1993, 1–2.

2. When Paul took his stance against Peter at Antioch, none of the others present seem to have joined him and he was left isolated. Cf. J. D. Dunn, *The Epistle to the Galatians*, London 1993, 12.

3. R. A. Cole sums up the argument succinctly: "One thing very clear on a plain reading of the letter to the Galatians is the use that Paul makes of Christian experience, as an argument. Whether it is an appeal to the experience of the Galatians before their conversion (4:8) or after their conversion (4:15), or to their experience of the Spirit both initially and continually at work in their midst (3:2–5), or to Paul's own experience at and after his own conversion (1:13–17), or to his experience in connection with the Jerusalem apostles (1:18–2:14), it is basically always the same argument." *Galatians,* Grand Rapids 1989, 45.

4. Cp. C. K. Barrett, *Paul, An Introduction to his Thought,* London 1994, 168.

5. Fitzmyer, 103–104.

6. J. Beker, *The Triumph of God: the Essence of Paul's Thought,* Minneapolis 1990, 135.

7. Cf. L. Cerfaux, *Christ in the Theology of St. Paul,* E. T. New York 1962.

Chapter Two

1. C. Stock, *Call to Discipleship: A Literary Study of Mark's Gospel,* Dublin 1982, 9, 73–74.

2. Malachy 2:13–16 is a reminder that in later Old Testament times divorce was not unanimously accepted.

3. There are resurrection appearances to the disciples in the present ending of Mark but Mark 16:9–20, known as the longer ending, is generally regarded by scholars today as a second-century addition. It differs in style and vocabulary from the rest of the Gospel and is absent from the earliest manuscripts.

4. J. D. Kingsbury, *Conflict in Mark,* Philadelphia 1989. My conclusion is based on pp.115–17.

Chapter Three

1. "Virtually all recent studies on Matthew's gospel would agree that this evangelist and his community have strong roots in Judaism and that Matthew's gospel was concerned with such Jewish issues as fidelity to the law and the destiny of God's people." D. Senior, *What are They Saying about Matthew?* New Jersey 1996, 19–20.

2. C. Deutsch, *Hidden Wisdom and the Easy Yoke,* Sheffield 1987, 41.

3. Deutsch, 42.

4. Deutsch, 135.

5. F. W. Beare, *The Gospel According to Matthew,* Oxford 1981, 125.

6. Senior, *What Are They Saying about Matthew?* 72.

7. Beare, 127.

8. Meier argues that the word *porneia* (unchastity) is not used by Matthew to signify adultery but means an incestuous union. *Matthew,* Dublin 1980, 52–53.

9. Meier, *Law and History in Matthew's Gospel,* Rome 1976, 168.

Chapter Four

1. Fitzmyer, *The Gospel According to Luke I–IX,* New York 1979, 287.

2. Fitzmyer, *The Gospel According to Luke I–IX,* 484.

3. Obviously, in the kind of scroll used in the synagogues of the time, these texts would not have been side by side. So we can see Luke's hand at work in the presentation of the episode.

4. Fitzmyer, *The Gospel According to Luke I–IX,* 247.

5. Fitzmyer, *The Gospel According to Luke I–IX*, 249–50.

6. J. B. Green, *Jesus of Nazareth: Lord and Christ*, Carlisle 1994, 59.

7. Green, 68. The author quotes a relevant injunction from the monastic community of Qumran. "In the Rule of the Congregation, the parameters of the con- vocation of the whole assembly are set, and they exclude those who are afflicted in the flesh, those with injured feet or hands, the lame, blind, crippled, and those with a permanent bodily defect or bodily impurity (1QM 7:4–6)," 69.

8. Fitzmyer, *The Gospel According to Luke I–IX*, 234.

9. R. Schnackenburg, *Jesus in the Gospels*, Louisville 1993, 207.

10. M. A. Powell, *What Are They Saying about Luke?* Mahwah, N. J. 1989, 96.

11. In his book *Biblical Reflections on Crises Facing the Church*, New York 1975, 84–108, R. Brown suggests that discipleship is the key to the interpretation of Mary in the New Testament. This explains the "remarkable plasticity of her image through the ages." (*The Birth of the Messiah*, London 1977, 318 n. 66.)

12. Filling in a story was a technique of Luke. "In the conversation between the risen Jesus and the two dis- ciples on the road to Emmaus, the discussion of the death and Resurrection of Jesus in terms of OT fulfill- ment (Luke 24:19–27) is simply a digest in conversa- tional form of the preaching of the early Church on this problem as Luke presents it in Acts." Brown, *The Birth of the Messiah*, 316 n. 57.

13. Brown, *The Birth of the Messiah*, 351.

14. "He had an excellent antecedent for this in the OT portrait of Hannah the mother of Samuel, a handmaid of the Lord who sang a hymn of the Anawim (1 Sam 1:11; 2:1–10)." Brown, *The Birth of the Messiah*, 357.

Chapter Five

1. Schnackenburg, *The Gospel According to John*, Vol. 3, New York 1982, 205.

2. Meier, unpublished lecture at All Hallows College, Dublin, November 4, 1997.

3. R. Bultmann, *The Gospel of John*, E. T. Philadelphia 1971, 530.

4. Brown, *The Gospel According to John*, Vol. 2, London 1971, 675.

5. J. Ashton, *Understanding the Fourth Gospel*, Oxford 1991, 208.

6. The reference to "the Jews" in chapter 9 and throughout John cannot be taken simply to mean the Jewish race as such. After all, Jesus and his disciples were Jews, as was the mother of Jesus and his family. In the fourth Gospel "the Jews" is best interpreted as a code word for those who resist the light of Christ's revelation. The choice of the expression is probably the result of disputes that took place between the early Christians and local Jewish synagogues. Cf. Ashton, *Understanding the Fourth Gospel*, 134–35.

7. For a detailed commentary on John 9 see Brown, *The Gospel According to John*, Vol. 1, London 1966, 371–82.

8. Cf. Y. Simoens, *Passion, Mort et Resurrection de Jesus Selon Jean 18–21*. Notes for auditors, Biblical Institute, Rome, 1996–97, 177.

Chapter Six

1. Simoens, *Passion Mort et Resurrection de Jesus Selon Jean 18–21*, 82.

2. Senior, *1 & 2 Peter*, Wilmington 1980, 27.

3. J. H. Elliott, *1 and 2 Peter*, Minneapolis 1982, 84. The

Anglican scholar J. N. D. Kelly echoes this opinion in *A Commentary on the Epistles of Peter and Jude*, London 1969, 98.

4. "And so in this passage of Revelation we are entitled to recognize not only one of the first testimonies to the veneration which the Church has, from a very early date, accorded to its martyrs and saints, but also the foundation for the piety which has led Christians from the earliest centuries to turn to them for their intercession. If they are priests with Christ and reign with him, it is certainly not useless to address ourselves to them." A. Vanhoye, *Old Testament Priesthood and the New Priest*, Petersham Mass. 1986, 305.

5. Brown, *Priest and Bishop, Biblical Reflections*, New York 1970, 68–69.

6. The other text is 4:7–11.

7. 1 Tim 3:1–7, Titus 1:6–9.

Chapter Seven

1. A poll conducted by *Time*/CNN found that 9% of people interviewed believed that the world as we know it would end in the year 2000. *Time* January 18, 1999, 46.

2. Meier, *A Marginal Jew*, Vol. 2, 31.

3. Meier, *A Marginal Jew*, Vol. 2, 349.

4. The structure and genre of Revelation are matters of some dispute. E. Fiorenza wonders what particular form the author had in mind. "Did he intend to create a liturgy or a drama, a cosmic myth, a prophetical book or an apocalypse? Or did he use all of these genres to fill out the epistolary framework which reflects his true literary intention?" "Composition and Structure of the Book of Revelation," *Catholic Biblical Quarterly*, 39 (1977): 350–51.

5. R. Baucham, *The Climax of Prophecy*, Edinburgh 1993, 176.

6. E. Fiorenza, *Revelation, Vision of a Just World*, Minneapolis 1991, 63.

7. C. H. Giblin, "Recapitulation and John's Apocalypse," *Catholic Biblical Quarterly*, 56 (1994): 94.

8. K. E. Miller considers chapters 19–22 as all part of the final marriage vision. The Rider who appears in 19:11–21 is about to usher in his "nuptial reign." Like the Bride, he too wears a wedding robe on which is written "King of Kings and Lord of Lords." "The Nuptial Eschatology of Revelation 19–22," *Catholic Biblical Quarterly*, 60 (1998): 301–18.

9. D. McIlraith, *The Reciprocal Love between Christ and the Church in the Apocalypse*, Rome 1989, 196.

10. L. L. Thompson, *The Book of Revelation*, Oxford 1990, 84.

11. M. Boring, "Narrative Christology in the Apocalypse," *Catholic Biblical Quarterly*, 54 (1992): 702–23.

12. Boring, 716.

References

Achtemeier, P. J., "'He Taught Them Many Things': Reflections on Marcan Christology," *Catholic Biblical Quarterly*, 42 (1980): 465–81.

Albright, W. F., and Mann, C. S., *Matthew*, New York 1971.

Allison, O. C., *The New Moses: A Matthean Typology*, Edinburgh 1993.

Anderson, H., *The Gospel of Mark*, London 1981.

Ashton, J., *Understanding the Fourth Gospel*, Oxford 1991.

———. *Studying John*, Oxford 1994.

Ball, D. M., *'I Am' in John's Gospel*, Sheffield 1996.

Barrett, C. K., *Paul, An Introduction to his Thought*, London 1994.

Baucham, R., *The Climax of Prophecy*, Edinburgh 1993.

Beare, F. W., *The Gospel According to Matthew*, Oxford 1981.

Beker, J. *The Triumph of God: the Essence of Paul's Thought*, Minneapolis 1990.

———. *Paul Apostle to the Gentiles*, E. T. Westminster 1993.

Brown, R. E., *The Gospel According to John*, Vol. 1 and Vol. 2, London 1966, 1971.

————. *Priest and Bishop, Biblical Reflections,* New York 1970.

————. *Biblical Reflections on Crises Facing the Church,* New York 1975.

————. *The Birth of the Messiah,* London 1977.

————. *The Community of the Beloved Disciple,* London 1979.

————. *The Death of the Messiah,* New York 1994.

————. *Introduction to the New Testament,* New York 1996.

Brown, R. E., and Meier, J., *Antioch and Rome,* New Jersey 1983.

Bruce, F. F., *The Epistle to the Hebrews,* Grand Rapids 1990.

Bultmann, R., *The Gospel of John,* E. T. Philadelphia 1971.

Carter, W., "Matthew 4:18–22 and Matthean Discipleship: An Audience-Oriented Perspective," *Catholic Biblical Quarterly,* 59 (1997): 58–75.

Cerfaux, L., *Christ in the Theology of St. Paul,* E. T. New York 1962.

Cole, R. A., *Galatians,* Grand Rapids 1989.

Collins, R. F., *These Things Have Been Written,* Louvain 1990.

Cosgrove, C. H., *The Cross and the Spirit,* Macon 1988.

Davis, C. A., *The Structure of Paul's Theology,* New York 1995.

Deutsch, C., *Hidden Wisdom and the Easy Yoke,* Sheffield 1987.

Dodd, C. H., *The Interpretation of the Fourth Gospel,* Cambridge 1970.

Donaldson, T. C., *Jesus on the Mountain,* Sheffield 1985.

Dunn, J. D., *The Epistle to the Galatians,* London 1993.

Elliott, J. H., *The Elect and the Holy,* Leiden 1966.

Fiorenza, E., *Revelation, Vision of a Just World,* Minneapolis 1991.

Fitzmyer, J., *Pauline Theology*, New Jersey 1967.

———. *The Gospel According to Luke I–IX*, New York 1979.

———. *According to Paul*, New York 1993.

———. *The Acts of the Apostles*, New York 1998.

Green, J. B., *Jesus of Nazareth: Lord and Christ*, Carlisle 1994.

Guelich, R., *The Sermon on the Mount*, Dallas 1982.

Gundry, R. H., *Mark: A Commentary on His Apology for the Cross*, Grand Rapids. 1993.

Hanson, A. T., *The Pastoral Epistles*, Grand Rapids 1982.

Hooker, M. D., *The Gospel According to Mark*, London 1991.

Kealy, S. P., *Mark's Gospel: a History of Its Interpretation*, New York 1982.

Kelly, J. N. D., *A Commentary on the Epistles of Peter and Jude*, London 1969.

Kingsbury, J. D., *The Christology of Mark's Gospel*, Philadelphia 1983.

———. *Matthew*, Philadelphia 1986.

———. *Matthew as Story*, Philadelphia 1988.

Leon-Dufour, X., *Lecture de L'Evangile selon Jesus*, Paris 1993.

Marshall, H., *The Gospel of Luke*, Exeter 1978.

Martyn, J. C., *History and Theology in the Fourth Gospel*, New York 1968.

McIlraith, D., *The Reciprocal Love between Christ and the Church in the Apocalypse*, Rome 1989.

Meier, J., *Law and History in Matthew's Gospel*, Rome 1976.

———. *Matthew*, Dublin 1980.

———. *The Mission of Christ and his Church*, Wilmington 1990.

———. *A Marginal Jew*, Vol. 1 and Vol. 2, New York 1991, 1994.

Michel, O., *The Interpretation of Matthew*, Edinburgh 1995.

Murphy-O'Connor, J., *Paul, A Critical Life*, Oxford 1996.

Penna, R., *Paul the Apostle: Wisdom and Folly of the Cross*, Vol. 2, Collegeville 1996.

Plevnik, J., "What is the Centre of Pauline Theology?" *Catholic Biblical Quarterly*, 51 (1989): 461–78.

Powell, M. A., *What Are They Saying about Luke?*, Mahwah, N. J. 1989.

Reid, B. E., *Choosing the Better Part?*, Collegeville 1996.

Richard, E., *Jesus: One and Many*, Wilmington 1988.

Richard, P., *Apocalypse*, New York 1995.

Richards, M., *A People of Priests*, London 1995.

Sanders, E. P., *Paul and Palestinian Judaism*, Philadelphia 1977.

Schnackenburg, R., *The Moral Teaching of the New Testament*, New York 1960.

———. *The Gospel According to John*, Vol. 3, New York 1982.

———. *Jesus in the Gospels*, E. T. Louisville 1993.

Senior, D., *1 & 2 Peter*, Wilmington 1980.

———. *What Are They Saying about Matthew?*, New Jersey 1996.

Simoens, Y., *Passion, Mort et Resurrection de Jesus Selon Jean 18–21*. Notes for auditors, Biblical Institute Rome, 1996–97.

Sloan, R. B., *The Favorable Year of the Lord*, Austin 1977.

Stock, C., *Call to Discipleship: A Literary Study of Mark's Gospel*, Dublin 1982.

Strecker, G., *The Sermon on the Mount*, E. T. Nashville 1988.

Talbert, C. H., *Reading Luke*, New York 1986.

Thompson, L. L., *The Book of Revelation*, Oxford 1990.

Trilling, E., *Das Warhe Israel*, Munich 1964.

Vanhoye, A., *Old Testament Priesthood and the New Priest,* E. T. Petersham, Mass. 1986.

Wenham, D., *Paul: Follower of Jesus or Founder of Christianity?*, Cambridge 1995.

Sheed & Ward

Other Books of Interest
available at your favorite bookstore

Faithful Listening
Discernment in Everyday Life
Joan Mueller
Read to fall in love with the Holy Spirit who moves us to better decisions and more balanced relationships. The difficulty of discerning choices is a basic unfamiliarity with the nature and process of discernment itself. Mueller remedies this with a textured overview of this practical charism of attending to God's Spirit.
140 pp 1-55612-900-9 *$14.95*

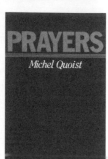

Prayers
Michel Quoist
A classic of modern spirituality. With simplicity and strength, this collection of powerful prayers will help you structure and develop your own sense of prayer. This assembly of petition and thanksgiving represents the full range of human emotion, from despair to mystical union. Drawn from the world around us, these prayers will enrich your relationship with God.
190 pp 0-934134-46-4 *$11.95*

Divine Designs
Exercises for Spiritual Growth
Rosemarie Carfagna
Nine areas that Christians are likely to pass through on their journey to personal holiness are highlighted. Movement through these stages is charted in practical terms. Suffering, Transformation, Dying, and Leading are included, along with ways to envision, hear, and enact growth and spiritual integration.
177 pp 1-55612-862-2 *$14.95*

Endless Connections
Taking God's Word to Heart
Jane Eschweiler, S.D.S.
An interplay between God's Word and the community's real experiences: marriage, potlucks, tragedy, sickness, and porch-sitting. Thoughtful insights that will touch your heart in poetic and unexpected ways. Ideal for anyone seeking new wisdom.
200 pp 1-55612-915-7 *$14.95*

 SHEED & WARD
An Apostolate of the Priests of the Sacred Heart

30 Amberwood Parkway

Email www.bookmasters.co   or *Fax* 419-281-6883